PRAISE FOR *Get A Life!*

"Randy focuses us upon Christ and reveals himself with vulnerability and warmth while giving practical and insightful reflections on the Ephesian's letter."

DOUG BURLEIGH, PRESIDENT, *Young Life*

"Randy encourages us to "get a life," and what a life it is! Using personal stories and sharp biblical insight, Rowland challenges us to take God at his word and follow him unconditionally. This book can help each of us live with more faith, joy, and passion!"

JOHN WESTFALL, AUTHOR OF
Coloring Outside the Lines

Get A Life!

...AND A FAITH THAT WORKS

*What an Early
Christian Community
Says to Us Today*

RANDY ROWLAND

HarperSanFrancisco
A Division of HarperCollinsPublishers

FIRST EDITION

Library of Congress Cataloging-in-Publication Data

Rowland, Randy.
Get a life! : . . .and a faith that works / Randy Rowland. — 1st ed.
    p. cm.
ISBN 0–06–066998–5 (acid free paper)
1. Bible. N.T. Ephesians—Criticism, interpretation, etc.
    2.Christian life—Biblical teaching. I. Title.
BS2695.2R68 1992   91-70038
227'.506—dc20   CIP

92 93 94 95 96 ❖ CWI 10 9 8 7 6 5 4 3 2 1

This edition is printed on acid-free paper that meets the American National Standards Institute Z39.48 Standard.

To my wife, Nancy, my daughter, Rachel, and my son, Andrew, and to all my friends and colleagues at University Presbyterian Church, especially Cornerstone Fellowship, who first endured my exploration of Ephesians.

Contents

Foreword

I am so glad my friend Randy Rowland has chosen Paul's letter to the Ephesians as the subject for his first book. It is one of my favorite books in the Bible. The scriptures provide a clear message of who we are as God's people, what we are to do, and how we are to live. And perhaps there is no place where that message is more clearly laid out for us than in Paul's letter to the Ephesians.

Someone has said we are quick to believe the incredible, while remaining skeptical about the everyday. Told that there are three hundred billion stars in the universe, we say, "of course." On the other hand, a simple sign saying "wet paint" tempts us to test its truth. I think the book of Ephesians invites us to make that kind of see-for-yourself test. Coleridge, the English poet, called Ephesians the most profound book in existence. Known as the "queen of the epistles," it stands alone as an overview—from God's perspective—of God's master plan for creation, for the church, and for us personally.

Unlike other Pauline epistles, the letter does not address one specific problem. Rather, Paul wrote in order to broaden the horizons of that infant church. He wanted them to understand, from God's perspective, that to which they had been called. He was alarmed by the political and ethical divisions in the early church. There was recurring conflict between the Jewish Christians and the Gentile Christians. Those who were formerly Jews kept most of their own religious forms—circumcision and the strict observance of the Sabbath and of dietary laws. The Gentile Christians refused to adopt those rules and regulations, insisting that the new covenant in Christ rendered the old Jewish laws and customs unnecessary.

In addressing this major division in the household of faith, Paul makes it clear that there is liberty and freedom in Jesus Christ, but he also emphasizes the universality and the unity made possible in Him. Throughout the epistle, the key word is *one. We are one; the Father is one with us; we are one with one another.* Together, we make up one body with one Lord, one faith, one baptism.

Sir Thomas Beecham, the eminent conductor of the London Symphony, often acted as guest conductor for other orchestras. On one occasion he was having a good deal of difficulty with a seemingly undisciplined group of musicians. During rehearsal, he was asked by the concert master how he wanted a particular section played. After a long pause and with great forbearance, he replied, "Together!" That's what Paul writes about in Ephesians—that individual Christian believers are called to do and be something together—to be, in fact, one.

Actually, Paul was attempting to lay out for those early church members God's master plan, and if we are unaware of that grand design, we can get lost on the faith journey. We may be like the guide who was hired by some hunters to take them into the back woods of Maine. After some days, they became hopelessly lost and quite naturally began to doubt the competence of their guide. "You said you were the best guide in Maine," they reminded him. "I am," he said, "but I think we're in Canada now." Theologically speaking, we can wander forever in a foreign land unless we understand the master design of our Creator, who, speaking through Paul, laid out his plans and purposes for the church.

It is God's plan that the church be the unifying force for *everything* in the world. It is a mindboggling mandate and one we need to take more seriously. The universities founded in the middle ages were constructed with the chapel at the center. Theology was considered the queen of sciences. The architecture of the time confirmed the prevailing belief that understanding the revelation of God in Jesus Christ was the beginning of all learning. Around that central focus were the buildings for mathematics, astronomy, chemistry, philosophy, and all the rest. All other disciplines were to revolve around the centrality of God as revealed in Jesus Christ.

Paul's advice to the Ephesians is especially relevant to the church in our time. Ephesus was a powerful and wealthy city, the center for culture and commerce. Its citizens were racially and ethnically diverse. Our own land, called for centuries a melting pot, has now become a mosaic of all kinds of religious, cultural, and ethnic groups. We Christians are a minority in our land as were the Christians at Ephesus. We, as they, are called to confront a largely pagan and materialistically motivated society.

Paul lived and worked in the city of Ephesus for two years. He lectured in a public hall for several hours a day and plied his tent making trade before and after those hours. Rabbis of his time were supposed to work for living. They were not remote and lofty scholars out of touch with the working people.

Randy Rowland has used Paul's example as a model for his own ministry. For many years he pursued what is called a tent making ministry. He is the first ordained tent maker in the Presbyterian Church—ordained to preach and teach without salary. He served the University Presbyterian Church in Seattle where I was senior pastor for ten years. Like the Apostle Paul, he supported himself.

In his ministry in Seattle, Randy has had an enormous impact on the babyboomer generation and through him radical changes have taken place in the lives of people who were living the "get rich and get ahead" lifestyle of our time.

Randy Rowland is a valued friend. I heartily endorse his book and recommend it to all who would read it. He exhorts us to get a life. But, not just any life—a life centered in Jesus Christ. It is the very message that Paul writes to the Ephesian church.

BRUCE LARSON

Acknowledgments

I am indebted to my family, especially my best friend and wife, Nancy, who encouraged me throughout the writing of this book. I cannot fail to mention my friend and daughter, Rachel, whose blue eyes and big smile make me feel like I could do anything. The love and support I receive at my house, even from our new son, Andrew, have put me on the road to discover all that God wants me to be.

I am also deeply grateful to my friends at University Presbyterian Church in Seattle, which has been the testing ground for most of this book's content. I extend special thanks to the Cornerstone Fellowship for inviting me to do the teaching series that stimulated the idea for this book, and to Rev. John Westfall, who has been a golf and racquetball buddy as well as a partner in ministry and a great inspiration. Darrel Young and Marianne Peirsol are co-workers for whom I have much love and respect. They, too, have been a great help to me in my dark moments. Suzanne Burgan is an excellent idea person and a faithful helper on projects; without her, I would be sunk.

Thanks as well to Bruce Larson and Doug Burleigh. These men are two great mentors and two great models for me. I love them dearly and pray that their investment in me is justified.

Introduction

Every now and then we have an awakening. A moment. We experience something that tells us all too clearly who we are. It's not always good news. I had such an experience several years ago on what I thought would be just another day. I was in Colorado Springs, standing in line at a ticket counter trying to negotiate a ticketing problem with an airline agent. He was rude and inflexible. I became terse and inflexible. Our conversation escalated into a full-blown war.

His fellow employees and my business partner had to intervene to prevent a fistfight. This was not a drunken barroom brawl between a couple of kids. This was two grown men. And one of them—myself—happens to be not only a person who calls himself a Christian, but someone who is an ordained minister.

In the moments following this battle, I was overcome by my lack of restraint. I possessed no power, no insight, no impulse to rise above the situation. I was cut loose from all emotional and moral moorings. I was a wheel spinning off its center—equipped only for destruction. I knew then, and am convinced now, that I desperately need a personal center. I need a sanctuary or reservoir within from which can flow my power for living.

What was wrong with the way I acted at the airport that day? I mean, beyond the obvious, that it didn't look good. Sure, my conscience was violated. But beyond that was the frightening reality that my whole life is on the edge of being out of control. My actions were merely a parable—a symbolic little story—about who I am.

I am a typical child of my generation—a baby boomer who has been from Beatlemania to disco beats to buying real estate and stock options looking for a meaningful life. I have survived the Hoola Hoop craze, streaking, and young urban professionalism in a quest to discover what really makes life meaningful. Like many other baby boomers, I've gotten glimpses of what life can be, yet there is always this sense that things aren't quite lined up right—a sense that life is off-center and may soon unravel.

Many of us are trying to find a center for life. We seek a source of strength, a pattern for integrity, and a strategy for purposeful living. Many are attempting to discover this center by sincerely investigating the Christian faith. Some have found that a spiritual relationship with Jesus Christ has begun to address some of the major issues in their lives. But most of us are struggling. We wonder how God, Bible, church, prayer, sacrifice, and service fit into the whole puzzle of life. We are curious about faith. Can belief in God be a truly transforming experience?

The heart of baby-boomer existence is the attempt to define and attain a quality of life worth living. What does it look like? How do we get it? What will it feel like? Can I do it quickly and painlessly? How will it affect my family and friends? Will I like it?

The boomers are not the first generation with questions. We are not the first generation for which the search for maximized life in the midst of prosperity and innumerable options is the key issue. Nearly two thousand years ago, there was a world-famous city in the Mediterranean of incredible wealth and enormous spiritual hunger. That city was called Ephesus.

Ephesus was a center of international trade. It was racially and ethnically diverse. It was economically vibrant but stressed by the weight of its success, like an overbearing peach tree whose branches are taxed by the abundance of fruit.

Doesn't this parallel late-twentieth-century America, where much of life focuses on economics and the success of complicated business relationships? And certainly we can relate to the prosperity that adds so many options to life that it becomes unbearably confusing. The Ephesians knew what it was to suffer with too much. They, like us, knew the feeling of the "full-plate" syndrome, where we simply overload on the buffet line of possibilities for life.

Ephesus was also a place of incredible diversity. The multicultural population left the stamp of many religions, philosophies, and life-styles on every aspect of life. We experience that as well. Our society is no longer a "melting pot." We have become a mosaic. The issue is no longer one of becoming "the same," but of living together in the midst of innumerable differences. We have no concrete societal norms that provide a clear center for living.

Ephesus was also a spiritual haven. This first-century city had it all—from philosophies of life to mystery religions that involved baths in blood and ecstatic dances that often left the participant mortally wounded at his or her own hand. In addition to these wild spiritualities, there were the Greco-Roman religions, Judaism, and fledgling Christianity. Many people weren't sure whether one religion was right, whether parts of all were right, or whether they were all wrong and their adherents just in it for the money. There was a temptation to not commit to a "core" or central faith to guide and motivate.

In Ephesus, the stress on families was enormous. The roles of wife, husband, mother, father, child, and slave were all in question. It was difficult to discern how key relationships and roles were to be lived out. The prevailing culture of the day placed high values and expectations upon roles. Yet those values and expectations were complex and confusing. For example, a family in Ephesus might have consisted of husband, wife, children, grandparents, servants, and perhaps even key members of the family business. The success and failure of the family was placed squarely on the shoulders of the husband, yet he might be out of town doing business over half of the year. Roles were thought of rigidly. That left the entire household in an unstable mode, with contingent lines of authority. The message of the gospel addressed these problems as "people" issues, not as role difficulties.

It isn't hard to see that our present society, particularly for those born between about 1946 and 1964, is very similar to that of Ephesus in the first century. Many of the Ephesians were just like the baby boomers. They had started coming to the Christian church in Ephesus, exploring the faith and looking for a meaningful and centered life. They were at various stages of growth. They were committed to discover something real and workable— or they would soon look elsewhere.

In the middle of the first century, less than forty years after Jesus Christ lived on earth, a remarkable man named Paul, who had had a personal encounter with Christ, wrote a letter to his friends in Ephesus. We own that letter today as a book in the New Testament called the Epistle (letter) to the Ephesians. It is an extraordinary letter—jammed with insights into the nature of life, faith, relationship, and engagement with the forces of this world and even unseen spiritual worlds. Most important, it contains the secrets to discovering meaning in life.

Ephesians is a book that works backward from the way most of us tend to think. While we seek to change our circumstances and our behaviors, the apostle Paul is concerned that we embark on a relationship with Jesus Christ. This relationship literally transforms our innermost person—our character. Such a change makes our behaviors a natural and congruent outflow from that center. As we are transformed internally, our ability to cope and adapt to life increases, and the circumstances of our lives (which are often a prime focus for us) become less important. Don't you dream of living beyond "If only I could . . ." or "When I get a new job and more money I'll . . ."? Ephesians offers the answers in clear and understandable form.

To a culture broken and dysfunctional by the force of its diversity and pace, Paul offers a centering understanding of grace— what it means to experience forgiveness and unconditional acceptance in a performance-oriented world.

To someone dying of loneliness in the midst of a crowd, Paul offers a new understanding of how our centered faith empowers us to have nurturing relationships. He explores living out relationships with new motives for loving and being loved and a fresh definition of intimacy. And to a self-serving people compelled to be consumers—little Pac-Men who lustily gobble up all that life has to offer in the hope of being fulfilled—Paul offers the joy of being motivated from the innermost person, armed and equipped to go beyond the self. He brings hope to a world dying to know what is really right, what is love, and how to live with confidence.

Ephesians is a letter about God's intent to "re-create" each of us. But there is more. Paul makes the bold claim that, in addition to attaining personal transformation, we can be partners with God in healing and restoring our world as we place Christ at the center of our personal lives. We participate with God in the re-creation process. As we live from the center, our very thoughts and actions are transformed. Our relationships take on a quality that transforms and lifts others. We find ourselves working as carpenters in God's re-creation. I find myself seeking to understand rude airline agents. Instead of going across the ticket counter in rage, I can envision myself so transformed that I no longer call another of God's children a profane name. Instead, I am not affected by his behavior—I am driven by my center.

The fact is that what we are at the core of our person colors all that we are and all that we do. We desire to discover a healthy and meaningful center. We desire to have what we are at the deepest level become a force that shapes who we want to be on the outside. Ephesians is a two-thousand-year-old letter that works as our modern road map for discovering the center for living.

I invite you to join me in an exciting adventure deep into an ancient text that will empower your life and mine today, tomorrow, and even into eternity.

PART
ONE

Introduction

We have all developed different ideas about who God is and what his intentions are for this world and the people in it. Early on in Ephesians, Paul makes it absolutely clear that the God and Father of our Lord Jesus Christ is all-loving and all-powerful. His intentions for us are good.

God is on our side. Further, God possesses resources that he lends to us so that we may become all that he dreams for us to be.

God wants to empower our lives to be meaningful, fulfilling, and productive. God is exercising the power of his Holy Spirit to re-create the universe in Christ, reversing the devastating effects of sin. God is in the process of re-creating relationships with himself, relationships among persons, relationships between people and society, and especially wholeness in relationship with our own self.

It all begins by encountering Jesus Christ, the living Lord, in the very center of our lives—deep in the core of our being.

A relationship with Jesus begins when we recognize that he is pursuing us in his love and that he is neither far away nor difficult to find. God, in Christ, invites us to be his guests on an eternal adventure.

1 Beggar's Banquet

Praise be to the God and Father of our Lord Jesus Christ, who has blessed us in the heavenly realms with every spiritual blessing in Christ. For he chose us in him before the creation of the world to be holy and blameless in his sight. In love he predestined us to be adopted as his sons through Jesus Christ, in accordance with his pleasure and will—to the praise of his glorious grace, which he has freely given us in the One he loves. In him we have redemption through his blood, the forgiveness of sins, in accordance with the riches of God's grace that he lavished on us with all wisdom and understanding. And he made known to us the mystery of his will according to his good pleasure, which he purposed in Christ, to be put into effect when the times will have reached their fulfillment—to bring all things in heaven and on earth together under one head, even Christ. In him we were also chosen, having been predestined according to the plan of him who works out everything in conformity with the purpose of his will, in order that we, who were the first to hope in Christ, might be for the praise of his glory. And you also were included in Christ when you heard the word of truth, the gospel of your salvation. Having believed, you were marked in him with a seal, the promised Holy Spirit, who is a deposit guaranteeing our inheritance until the redemption of those who are God's possession—to the praise of his glory.

EPHESIANS 1:3-14

I remember a Rolling Stones album that was released during my teenage years. It was entitled *Beggar's Banquet*. The title had a real ring to it. I often wondered what the album title meant. I could never find a proper situation to which I could apply the term. Then, in the early seventies as I began to develop a Christian faith, I came across Ephesians 1:3–14.

The author of the passage is the apostle Paul. He is writing from prison in Rome, where he will soon pay for his faith with his very life. He is facing execution. Yet in the midst of all his discomfort, he had a relationship with God whose love and affirmation nourished him in spite of his circumstances. Somehow, he was sustained by his deep and centering relationship with God. He was enjoying a feast of God's blessings that by his own admission was both undeserved and unattainable by human effort. Paul did not view himself as a victim of the Roman justice system or some cruel act of fate. Rather, he saw himself as a participant in God's plan for the world. In the midst of circumstances that I cannot imagine enduring, Paul felt sincerely blessed and at peace. He was actually enriched by adversity. Paul was describing a beggar's banquet! Paul experienced a love so strong, so fundamental to who he was, that he was convinced of God's intention for each of us to live with that same love that comes from God at the center of our lives. In fact, Paul was sure that this love experience was so vital to who we are as people that God actually designed it to exist even before he built this world in which we live. That brings up the whole issue of predestination. What is the practical implication of the fact that "in love he predestined us "?

Many readers are thrown off by the mention of predestination in this passage of Scripture. They assume that this reading is strictly for Calvinists. Not so.

Imagine with me for a minute that you have guests coming to stay with you. They are your German relatives. You have spent days and weeks planning for their arrival, fixing up your home to welcome them. In addition, you have made an itinerary for their stay, scheduling the time you'll have together to show off the region in which you live. You have planned social, sports, cultural, and sightseeing events for them. You have lovingly shopped for foods that other relatives have informed you will suit their palates. You have even labeled areas of the house with signs bearing international symbols so that they will find your home comfortable. You have done everything to prepare for the likelihood of an outstanding visit.

Now, the fact remains that you and your relatives speak two different languages, and neither is conversational outside of his or her mother tongue. But you know a few words of German, and it will be obvious to those relatives by the way you have prepared for their stay that your love toward them is immense.

On the day of their arrival, you go to the airport in anticipation, and they arrive at the airport filled with excitement, fear, worries about cultural differences, and all the rest. But they are met and overwhelmed by your love. They see the signs in your home; they taste the familiar food. They see a schedule complete with pictures of where they will be visiting and are certainly assured of a peak experience.

You see, God has always loved us and desired that we be a part of his family even if some striking cultural differences and language barriers exist between us.

Here's what I mean about barriers. God is without limits in time, space, intelligence, and power. We, on the other hand, are quite limited. Because God is without limits, he can compute things like infinity, eternity, absolute zero, and other concepts beyond our capabilities. He cannot communicate to us in those terms. It's useless. That's why God "condescends" to us. Like a parent with an infant, God does baby talk so that we can understand. God uses tangible examples such as Jesus, the Son of God, becoming human so that we can relate to God on a more familiar basis. Some theologians have referred to Jesus as "God wearing a human costume."

God, you see, has gone out of his way to shower us with his love and to demonstrate that his plans for us are good. Repeatedly and in many ways he has shown us that he is on our side. He beckons us to discover a centering spirituality that connects us with him— a relationship wherein we begin to understand God, ourselves, and our world.

How has he beckoned us? Well, God himself visited the planet that he loves and longs to be in relationship with in the person of Jesus Christ. Jesus was God wearing a human mask. He approaches us in love and identifies with every part of the human condition, even the dark underside of humanity—all the things that we think we ought to hide from God. Jesus fully comprehended human fear, greed, temptation, compulsion, ambition, pride, prejudice, presumptuousness, and all the other aspects of the human condition. God knows who we are. That's good news! Even better news is that he likes us—and loves us completely as we are.

God does not come to us, though, just to make contact and check us out to see if we are fit to be called his friends. He is much more aggressive than that. He pursues us with his love. He has predestined that we have a desire to know him deep within us—at the center. He has made his plans known. In Jesus Christ, God has made the statement that he is in the business of "bring[ing] all things . . . together." That's his plan. God has told us ahead of time what he intends to do. He intends to intensely love all the world and bring all persons—in fact, all of creation—together in one New Family. That is the nature of predestination. It is a big and confusing theological word that simply means: God has gone ahead of us and set the stage for us to see his love, belong to him, and participate in his plan. Does that mean that everyone responds? Unfortunately, no.

Let's go back to my example of your imaginary relatives visiting from Europe. Is it possible that some members of that family might be snobbish and reject your attempts to make them feel at home? Of course that is a possibility. And, frankly, since the universe runs on free will, you might find that there is nothing you can do, no overture you can make that will cause those snobbish relatives to respond. In fact, they may sit in their rooms at your home for the entire stay, reading books and magazines that they have lugged from home, and never experience anything of your country. Being fully welcomed and having had the way paved for a great adventure, they simply reject the offer and continue to live as they always have, irrespective of their new location.

It is the same with us. All of us have had a road to God paved by the love of God himself expressed in Jesus Christ. No one can force us to take the road that was built for the very purpose of bringing us to God. If we refuse to travel that road, we remain as we are and where we are. That does not deny the reality of God's seeking us vigorously with his love and mercy; it simply reinforces the fact that we are unwilling to accept that which is provided for us.

So, a beggar's banquet awaits each of us. God has laid out the way to himself for us and has offered us every spiritual blessing that there is. That is, God has offered us every opportunity to attain our potential—to become members of his family and be empowered to live life to the absolute maximum. What an offer!

Another reason I think of these opening verses of Ephesians as a beggar's banquet is that they clearly establish that everything we attain spiritually—every benefit of being in relationship to God—is a gift. There is nothing we can do to earn this gift. God simply chooses in his love to lavish his resources upon us. So, as we encounter others in our lives who do not know of God's love and care for each human being, we are constrained to behave as one beggar speaking to another and tell where we have found bread. We don't have to tell others all about God. We needn't tell them what is wrong with their lives and what they have to do to get God on their side. We are free instead to simply tell our own story of encountering God's grace. We tell our story of how we have found a new center or focal point for living.

Bruce Larson, a well-known pastor and author, has been a tremendous influence on me and many others. He has a wonderful way of getting you to see things in a fresh light. In his sermons and books, Bruce often talks about the apostle Paul. One thing he has noted is that Paul sticks to his story. When asked to "hold court" and tell all about God, Paul simply discloses that while he was traveling to Damascus, as a Jewish leader on his way to kill Christians, he had an encounter with the resurrected Jesus that left him devastated. He reports being so overwhelmed by God's love that he was converted instantly, and the startling light of the revelation of Jesus Christ was so intense and real that he was even rendered physically blind for a short time. Paul knew he was privy to a beggar's banquet. He had little to boast about. All he could do was tell his story.

Your story of how you first came to know that God loved you and how your faith has grown to be more and more central in your life is a transforming story that will bring others to the banquet.

Paul says that God approaches us and the business of our lives "with all wisdom and understanding." The original Greek text of this passage could also be translated as "with all knowledge and intelligence." I think this is a wonderful concept. I don't want anyone who is not knowledgeable, who doesn't know how to read and interpret all the facts, messing with my life. And I am equally enamored by the fact that God, who made the whole universe, is the ultimate in intelligence.

Not only can God interpret the facts of my life accurately, he is the ultimate intelligence for designing a blueprint to put me together. God knows me inside out better than any human being ever will. It makes sense to trust him to empower me and encourage me to be all that I can be. As I focus and center myself in God's love and allow his Spirit to transform me, I discover increasing wholeness in my external life.

As I mentioned earlier, for me the key in this opening passage, the part that sets the stage for the entire letter to the Ephesians, is Paul's statement that God's purpose is to bring all things together. It doesn't take much looking around to see that we are living in a deeply broken world.

Our natural environment is threatened to the extent that ecology will be one of our major preoccupations for the next several decades. God wants to fix it.

People are feeling alienated; families are having a hard time surviving intact; marriages are fragile. God wants to fix the brokenness and bring "all things together"—even relationships.

People in our world today are anxious, stressed out, depressed, frustrated, and angry at depths never known before, more of the time than ever before in the history of humankind. Research says we are consuming aspirin at record rates to ease the pains of stress . . . which might in fact be existential pain. Technology is moving faster than we can absorb it. The pace is just too much for many of us. We feel exhausted, burned out, and broken. God wants to fix individuals, too. He wants to reintegrate us and bring us to a wholeness we have never known and cannot know apart from him.

People are living lives of hopelessness and despair. They are functional nihilists as they live separated from God—devoid of spiritual roots, resources, or worldviews. God wants to fix that, too. He is in the business of bringing "all things together," which means reuniting creature and Creator. Ephesians is the great story of re-creation—the universe is getting a make-over.

It begins at the center of our individual lives and radiates outward.

The final piece of Good News in this opening passage occurs when Paul notes that we don't live out our lives in a vacuum. We can live full of God's spirit. We can know God is alive. We can know God is with us. In fact, we can sense his presence—the presence of the Holy Spirit—and we can trust that presence as a guarantee that God really is at work re-creating a ruined world and reestablishing relationships that will one day bring the entire universe back into harmony. The Spirit's presence is our guarantee.

Assured of God's good intentions for us, encouraged by his presence, and working in partnership with him in the creation, we can live a life that is meaningful and filled with joy. Having set the stage for an adventure in Ephesians, we can now move on in this section and look more closely at the character of the One who invites us to be his family members. We can also begin to discover the resources he gives us to have a faith that works.

2

God
Calling

For this reason, ever since I heard about your
faith in the Lord Jesus and your love for all the
saints, I have not stopped giving thanks for you,
remembering you in my prayers. I keep asking
that the God of our Lord Jesus Christ, the glorious Father, may give you the Spirit of wisdom
and revelation, so that you may know him better. I pray also that the eyes of your heart may
be enlightened in order that you may know the
hope to which he has called you, the riches of
his glorious inheritance in the saints.

EPHESIANS 1:15-17

I may be telling a little too much about myself here as I confess
that I find some of the best philosophical insights written on
walls, appearing as lyrics, or on the comics page of my local
newspaper. One particular cartoon strip struck me so much recently that I cut it out and stuck it on my wall.

Lucy and Charlie Brown are conversing in a *Peanuts* strip.
Charlie has availed himself of Lucy's "psychological help" in her
backyard booth since she has marked down her rate from twenty-
five cents to a nickel per hour.

Lucy opens the dialogue something like this, "Charlie Brown,
life is like a cruise ship. On the cruise ship of life there are deck
chairs you can move around." Charlie focuses in as she continues,

"Some people take their deck chairs and place them on the front of the ship. They are hopeful. They always want to see where they are going. Others find comfort in the past and they like to put their deck chairs on the stern of the ship." Then the big question, "Charlie Brown, on the cruise ship of life, where would you put your chair?"

Charlie's face gets that wrinkled look that Charles Schulz made famous and he replies, "I just can't seem to get my deck chair unfolded."

I can sure relate to Charlie! Many of us can. A biblical text says that "we see but a poor reflection" (1 Cor. 13:12). Each of us catches glimpses of life and its meaning. We get an occasional sense of having it all together, but much of our time is spent trying to get our deck chairs unfolded—trying to make sense of the myriad of experiences, the waves of emotions that make up our lives. Most of us feel that there is too little time left to figure out all we need to know about ourselves and our world to make life a workable and fulfilling experience. Most of us feel disconnected. We sense that we desperately need but lack a center. For most of us, this is not an experience of a "past life"—we have felt this way even though we profess a pretty firm belief in God. Maybe we have claimed to be Christians all our lives. That doesn't make any difference. If you and I haven't grasped this idea of being alive from the inside out by a spiritual relationship with Jesus Christ, we may be running only on spiritual fumes while our tank is virtually empty. We're making the trip without the fuel to go the distance.

Recent polls have confirmed that the majority of Americans believe in God. A good number even believe that a connection with the Creator is made through Jesus Christ. Yet, there seems to be a great disparity between some of our religious sentiments and our fulfillment in life. Belief and experience don't seem to match up. Depression, adjustment reactions, chronic illness, and unmanageable levels of stress permeate our daily lives. It is apparent that something is wrong.

Some of us wonder if there is a God and, if there is and he does love us, why our relationship with him doesn't make a difference in our lives. Well, there is probably no simple answer to that question, but I am convinced that there are some age-old and often ignored biblical insights that can help each of us develop a faith that works. I believe we all long for that kind of faith. We all desire a spiritual experience that is integrated into the very fabric of our day-to-day existence.

The reason most of us have not had such an experience is that we are unwilling to go through the pain and struggle necessary to be free, functioning, and healthy. We tend to look for shortcuts, for pain-free solutions to the issues that haunt our innermost being. Then, when we find we can't be healed instantly by a book or a plan or a technique, we tend to give up and go back to the old and familiar pain. This is the disease of the baby-boomer generation. Instant gratification has instantly provided us with permanent frustration, disillusionment, and anxiety. Our operational mode has become external; we look for the "quick fix." If we are going to make it to the finish line in one piece and be able to say we enjoyed the race, we have to start investing in long-term solutions to our deepest struggles and needs. We must start at the heart of our being.

The opening line of M. Scott Peck's book, *The Road Less Travelled,* says, "Life is difficult." I don't necessarily like hearing the truth, but there is relief in discovering and accepting what is real. The fact is that life is difficult and change is difficult. It is also true that most of us don't change until we hurt badly enough.

Part of the pain of change is the uncertainty and risk that we feel as we reconstruct the way we respond to external influences. The reconstruction process is a learning process. It's slow. It's uncertain. It's threatening. It's painful.

One of my most significant personal experiences of how painful the learning process can be came during a college course in finance. The professor was a self-proclaimed tyrant. The course seemed impossible to pass and Dr. Strangebusiness was constantly affirming that fact. Five weeks into the twelve-week course, I had not a clue about the meaning of the lectures, reading, and classroom discussion. I barely survived the first midterm. At eight or nine weeks I was pretty sure that I understood what I was supposed to know at the end of week five. Finals were coming. Headaches, panic, depression, and throbbing anxiety were my daily companions. I was in a study group for the class, and most of our time studying was spent trying to keep each other alive emotionally and get the week's assignment done.

One of our group members was prone to just give up trying and start crying. Her math was good, but she needed the rest of us to keep her pumped up. Another fellow was an avid skier whose mind would occasionally take a chair lift to the top of the slope. I was hopelessly in love with a young lady I later married and could hardly concentrate myself. The only really together person in our group was a woman who had done accounting and finance for her dad's business while in high school. But she had chronic allergies and sneezed and blew her nose during much of our meeting time. What a crew! We really struggled.

Finals arrived way sooner than I would have liked, but I was ready. As if a light had come on instantly, the whole discipline of managerial finance opened up to me and I understood it. The final exam wasn't easy, but I got a solid grade in the course and to this day appreciate what I learned.

The learning process for my finance class and the learning processes that I have gone through in life are very similar. There is always great anguish and uncertainty at the beginning. My self-esteem ebbs to a new low in the throes of change and growth. But, on the upside, there always seems to be a concluding point of revelation and understanding that arrives suddenly and unexpectedly, tying the struggle together in one fairly cohesive whole. I always discover that with God's help I have taken a step forward . . . and that faith makes sense in a new and relevant way.

We can have a faith that works. Such a faith includes trust in God's character, belief in the Bible, and a personal relationship with Jesus Christ. These are the elements that facilitate an integrated faith, one involving the whole person. But we must be willing to bring that faith to several facets of our lives.

When I talk about integrated faith, I mean a faith that reaches deep inside a person. I mean a force that shapes that person's very core. I am talking about a faith that has the power to express itself consistently and progressively in outward behavior. I am talking about a faith that would prevent me from chewing out the man at the airline service counter. The faith that I am seeking to develop in my life has the possibility of transforming a variety of social, occupational, family, and self-management situations. This kind of faith is slow to form but sure to transform. It's hard to see developing but impossible to miss once it has taken root. I believe that it is the sort of faith that all of us long to possess and be empowered by.

Faith is like a delicate flower. It is slow to sprout and almost imperceptible in its growth—until finally it becomes something magnificent. Unfortunately, we get too hung up on the magnificent and become frustrated by the arduous process.

I liken faith development to my first experience with a personal computer. My wife, Nancy, and I had heard how wonderful computers were and how much they could do, so we did a little research and then used up the remaining credit on two charge cards to buy one. The proud computer owners came home and set up the machine, plugged it in, and turned it on. I fantasized that it would just write my next seminary paper for me. Wrong. I had to get acquainted with the computer before I could access its great power, speed, and flexibility.

Mastering the computer came slowly. It was a process. I probably could have saved more time on the first term paper I wrote on it by just hand typing the thing. But I stayed with the tedious process of learning to use the word processor. Later I learned

financial spreadsheets. Now, I couldn't function without the con-
venience of a PC. I never want to go back to the old way of typing
page after page and not being able to alter or insert ideas. I think
the thing that made me stay with my computer was that I had
gained a perspective from others with experience in computing
and believed that all my trials would be worth it. I saw the "end"
before I began.

Developing a solid, centered faith is much the same. We need
the experience of the apostle Paul, older friends, and key leaders
in our lives to help us see the end as we are beginning.

We need to have a perspective or a vision of what wholeness and
fulfillment are. In terms of our faith and our lives, I don't think
those of us in the 1990s differ too much from some of the earliest
Christians described in the New Testament. They had a firm basic
belief in God. They lived out their faith practically by reaching
out to their community and to the world. It was evident that God
was with this group of Christians.

The apostle Paul wrote a letter to one group of wealthy, worldly,
well-educated, and well-traveled Christians in a booming city on
the Mediterranean. That letter made it to the New Testament as
Ephesians. Paul acknowledges their well-founded faith but also
hints that they may be missing the essence of life as it was meant
to be. Paul seemed to believe there was an even more genuine experience of abundant life in Christ than the Ephesians were living
at the time he wrote his letter. Early in his correspondence, Paul
prays for the Ephesian Christians to begin a process of fully inte-
grating their Christian faith into daily life. Paul says, "I keep asking
that the God of our Lord Jesus Christ, the glorious Father, may give
you the Spirit of wisdom and revelation, so that you may know
him better." To know God "better" means to experience God's
presence in every aspect of our daily lives. Paul is talking about
knowing God so intimately that we possess God's perspectives on
life.

Paul understood that all people have a place for belief in God
in the core of their lives. Paul knew that personal fulfillment and

personal effectiveness are inextricably tied to knowing God. Paul was sure that all human beings are dependent upon receiving personal worth and direction from the Creator. He prays that every seeker and pilgrim in the faith will be able to say, "I want to know God better. I want to be a complete person spiritually, physically, intellectually, and emotionally." Paul is asking God to give the Ephesians a glimpse of what whole-person faith looks like.

The first part of Paul's prayer is for insight, or perspective. He prays for wisdom and revelation. He wants the Ephesians to understand that the exhausting process of seeking growth in their whole person will be worth the cost—just as learning to use my computer was worth the cost.

I find it fascinating that the first thing on our friend Paul's agenda is a plea for the Ephesians to develop insights about life that will make them want to get to know God better. This style really runs against the grain of our contemporary society's ambition to have it all now, to focus on results, to live for the moment.

This prevailing wind of philosophy is also well entrenched in our churches, where "Christian Growth by the Numbers" and "How to Get God to Answer Your Prayers" seminars are popular and financially profitable. Paul prays that God will give the Ephesians the needed vision and perspective for life first. He assumes that godly behaviors will follow. The true focus of my life should be on getting to know God better. That would solve most of my problems.

Paul glimpses God's dream for us and prays for it to become a reality. He asks that we would have insight into who God is and the mystery of how God works in our lives. Paul's prayer is that believers in Ephesus would encounter the Holy Spirit in a life-changing manner. If I could see life from God's perspective because of continually living in his presence, I would be a new person. I would live powerfully in the present, knowing that I was not seeing life just from my limited vista but from God's eternal vantage point.

We have many different theologies and perspectives on the Holy Spirit in our Christian churches today, but very few people would disagree that when someone acknowledges that she or he is a child of God, and that her or his life belongs to God, the Holy Spirit mysteriously enters that person's life at the deepest level and makes that person a new creation. The fact of the Spirit's presence is true whether you have believed in Christ ever since you can remember, grew into faith in Christ slowly, or met the Savior in some cataclysmic moment through a Billy Graham crusade or among a group of friends who shared the Good News with you on a college campus somewhere. The Holy Spirit dwells in every believer and works as a catalyst in the process of personal and spiritual growth.

Paul's words to a group of Christians in Philippi say, "I am *sure* that God who began a good work in you will continue it until the day of Jesus Christ" (Phil. 1:6). One of our common mistakes is that we somehow think that the Spirit goes to work on the exterior junk in our lives and ignores our innermost needs and concerns.

That isn't so. God begins at the center of our person and works toward the outside. Yes, as we come to Christ some outward habits may change dramatically because they are so threatening to ourselves or others that they are changed immediately. But most of us don't notice a dramatic change. Instead, we experience the frustration of not changing noticeably on the outside and not knowing what's happening on the inside. We may throw our hands up in frustration, thinking that our faith just isn't relevant to the nitty-gritty aspects of our lives.

The fact is that God cares immensely about the inner quality of our lives. He is at work in us through the Holy Spirit. This brings us to an important conclusion about spiritual and personal growth, which is that spiritual and personal growth are driven by two things: increased knowledge of self and increased knowledge of God. The two go hand in hand.

In the opening of his prayer for the Ephesians and for us, Paul asks for wisdom and revelation. Wisdom is the accumulation of knowledge about ourselves and about the human condition. But more than just knowledge of these things, it is an ability to inter-relate and sort that knowledge in a way that is applicable to specific events. Wisdom guides us in making good decisions. Although most of us don't like to go to a professional for help, sometimes we need to. Consider the person who goes to the doctor and asks for treatment for a skin abrasion while withholding from the doctor symptoms of fatigue and bone pain that might indicate the presence of leukemia. Wisdom would cause most of us to divulge all the probable symptoms, even if we were fearful of the results. One of the important things about wisdom is that it helps us face reality and avoid denial.

Wisdom is understanding and telling the truth about who we are as people and facing our need for help to become all that we can be. It also means a confession of our need for love. At the same time, wisdom doesn't let us shirk our responsibility to be a part of the process of becoming all that God dreams for us.

Revelation is a different matter. I know the word *revelation* is loaded. We have many diverse concepts and recollections of the word. But it doesn't have to be spooky. Revelation is the process of becoming increasingly aware that God is able and willing to speak to us. Revelation is a result of experiencing God's presence. Revelation is receiving sometimes subtle messages from God directly to us through our reflective acts of prayer, meditation, and study of Scripture. Revelation also comes to us through our inner emotional experiences with self. Revelation can come to us through our experiences with people we care about and the world as a whole.

I was recently evaluated on my leadership style by a group of people that I lead. They saw me as a very strong "seller"—a salesman. Much about the selling attributes is good. One thing is bad. A salesman always has an agenda and always fights against the answer "no." This was a revelation to me. I realized that my selling style characterizes how I approach God. I often have in mind just what he can do for me. I let him know. I persist. Even when the Spirit and circumstances appear to say "no," I try to negotiate or manipulate a "yes." I am learning to hear "no" and accept it.

Revelation can come internally through past experiences. Not too long ago I faced being fired from a job. I knew it was coming because of the company's poor profit picture. I had been fired from another job for almost the same reasons ten years before, so I wasn't a complete stranger to the experience of "termination."

Ten years before this most recent experience I had been fired from a church staff. My first firing was devastating. It cut me to the core. I was bitter, hurt, and angry. "Why me?" was my favorite sentence. I must confess that I loathe rejection, need to be needed, and am a terminally insecure person. Losing my important job laid raw all the fears and anxieties that are at the heart of my deepest, most secret needs. But out of that first experience I discovered a new career in broadcasting. My career as an announcer lasted a decade and allowed me to meet some of the most interesting music, news, and sports personalities in the world. It was a wonderful upside to a terribly threatening situation. I thank God for what happened.

Well, to get back to the most recent firing, I knew it was inevitable and I sensed through knowing who I am (morsel of wisdom) that this was going to be a difficult time. But I also had a deep confidence that God was in the midst of the situation (revelation) just as he was before, even though I had failed to recognize it back then.

When firing day came, I accepted my severance check, turned in my key, and cleaned out my office without much remorse. I somehow knew that God was opening new horizons, new ways for me to learn and grow through the change. Sure, I am human like everybody else—I was disappointed to be told that I was no longer needed. Several years down the road, however, I am grateful for the firing. My new career as a communications consultant and video producer with time to write and be involved in significant Christian ministry has been a tremendous experience. I have been challenged in new ways. On the other hand, I have had new fears uncovered and new issues to deal with. But I know that God is with me in it all. I am finding wisdom and revelation by way of the Holy Spirit!

Paul prays for all this wisdom and revelation. He says in this passage that it comes through the eyes of our heart. I thought this was an interesting phrase, so I looked it up in a book of word origins. For the first-century Greeks, the heart (*kardia* is the word) was thought to be the center of the intellect, the emotions, and the will. So when you saw something with the eyes of your heart and grabbed it, it grabbed your whole person. It grabbed the way you felt, it grabbed the way you thought, and it grabbed the way you behaved. It got all of you. What Paul is saying is that we can begin to see God at work in the world and at work in our lives in a way that grabs all of us—from the deepest level, in an integrated way.

Paul is praying that we gain the kind of knowledge that puts our spiritual experience to the test at that whole-person level that makes us genuine. Not long ago I was studying a passage of Scripture. In Philippians 1:10 (a parallel passage to this one in Ephesians), Paul prays for Christians to be "pure and blameless." The word for "blameless" in Greek means "sun-tested." It was a business term in those days when statues were put in the sun to test their worth.

There were many sculptures made and sold in those days, and sometimes a sculptor would accidentally put a nick in the material that he was carving. If any of you are sculptors you know that if you put a nick in something, often you've ruined the whole project and must start over again. To save himself from having to do that, a shoddy sculptor would fill in the crack with wax and then glaze the statue so that it appeared normal. Then, he'd wait for some chump to come and buy it even though it was broken. A smart person in those days would take any statue he wanted to buy, put it out in the noonday sun, and let the sun beat down on it for a while. If there was any inferior work, the heat of the sun and the light of day would send the wax dripping down the side of the statue and reveal the true quality of the sculpture. It wasn't genuine, blameless, or perfect. You see, that is the quality of life that God is trying to create in us; he wants us to become the kind of people who, when exposed to the harshness of life, set right out in the light of day, can take the heat—genuine people who don't melt down.

Part of being a whole person is admitting our "unwholeness." To stay with the sculptor analogy from Philippians, being integrated and whole means not making any effort to wax and glaze over our nicks and cracks, but rather to wear them up front.

In essence, then, spiritual growth is not simply a process of gathering more information about God or theology. We grow spiritually and personally in a context of knowing God. Growth is experiential. I need to know more about God and more about myself. Something mysterious happens as we grow comfortable in a deepening relationship with a severely flawed self and a flawless creator God. It is then that we have the courage to live by a faith that makes a difference.

3 Faith That Works

I pray also that the eyes of your heart may be enlightened in order that you may know the hope to which he has called you, the riches of his glorious inheritance in the saints, and his incomparably great power for us who believe. That power is like the working of his mighty strength, which he exerted in Christ when he raised him from the dead and seated him at his right hand in the heavenly realms, far above all rule and authority, power and dominion, and every title that can be given, not only in the present age but also in the one to come. And God placed all things under his feet and appointed him to be head over everything for the church, which is his body, the fullness of him who fills everything in every way.

EPHESIANS 1:18-23

There was a point in my life when I was pretty down. I had bill collectors calling me just about every day. They're tough people—bill collectors. "We need the seventy-five dollars for your gas bill." "I don't have seventy-five dollars." "You must give us seventy-five dollars." What a terrible guilty feeling. I felt like I had nothing, but I was getting less all the time. Here's a true story that I wouldn't believe if I hadn't been there.

I was down to two pairs of shoes and one of them was a pair of hiking boots. One day, I discovered that my hiking boots were gone. At the time, I was living with a family who had taken me in out of pure love. My monthly salary was about three hundred dollars less than my monthly bills. It was pretty bad. The four-year-old daughter of this family, Tina, came to me and sat on my lap and said, "Have you prayed to Jesus that you'll get your boots back and that God will take care of your problems with money? Mom and Dad said that's why you're sad today."

When a four-year-old asks you to pray to Jesus, you just do it! So Tina and her mom and I prayed together, and Tina prayed that God would bring my boots back. Only a few minutes later, a huge dog walked into the yard with my boots, tied together at the laces, hanging out of his mouth. He dropped them on the porch and walked away. It was the neighbor's dog that lived up the road in this rural area. He had somehow found my boots, picked them up, and brought them back to where they belonged and then gone on about his business. I told you it was a story that isn't easy to believe . . . but it happened.

Now, I don't want to trivialize the way that God answers prayer, nor do I wish to suggest that miraculous events like this happen every day. I do believe in the supernatural, though, and this is one of the few times I can say I have seen something so dramatically supernatural occur. But I think life itself is a miracle, and what I want to say is that God is powerful on our behalf. God works in the now. Sometimes when we get backed against the wall, when nothing else will work, God is willing to strengthen and comfort us by answering even the most trivial prayer.

My experience of distress with the missing hiking boots and the "miracle dog" has been a parable of the life of faith for me. When our resources are exhausted, God is willing to jump in. At the place where we have fully extended ourselves, God acts in our lives to bring hope to hopeless situations both big and small. To me, this is the essence of a faith that works—to have God make a demonstrable difference in our everyday lives, to have God be active in the now.

Paul's letter to the Ephesians offers us insights here. He continues his prayer, focusing now on three critical issues that will make or break followers of Christ as they seek an integrated faith. Paul says, "I pray also that the eyes of your heart may be enlightened in order that you may know the hope to which he has called you, the riches of his glorious inheritance in the saints, and his incomparably great power for us who believe. That power is like the working of his mighty strength, which he exerted in Christ when he raised him from the dead." Hope, inheritance, and power are the focus of Paul's thoughts.

Not long ago a dear friend and I had lunch together. Every time I visit with him I walk away with what I call a "ruby"—a real insight. This conversation was no different. We were discussing the difficulty of discovering God's will for our lives and he said, "God is always hidden in the now." His point was that we can look back in life, over our shoulder, and say, "Oh, God was in that." We can see God in our history, but oftentimes he seems mysteriously silent in our struggle to know and do what is right today.

I worry about some of the "pop" spirituality that is peddled on television and radio and in books. I even worry about what we get in some of the fellowship groups we attend. I am concerned about people who say, "Well, God's telling me to do this right now" as if, somehow, they've got God in their back pocket. That's not how life and faith really work. Most of us can't spot God in the moment and we don't know what's going on in the difficult times. We honestly ask God and others, "Why did this awful thing happen to me?" Then we are made to feel guilty and unspiritual and like we don't even know God by the media gurus of textbook faith.

I'm not rejecting you as a person if you've been a subscriber to those views. I'm just asking you to take a second look. *Is* that really God you're seeing in your present circumstances, or are you maybe being a little cocky or simplistic and overconfident? I think we need to be tough on ourselves and ask these sorts of questions lest we become presumptuous.

I'm not saying that God doesn't work in the present. He is at work all the time. I'm just not so sure that we are always able to see his hand as it is working. Sometimes we need to hold off on presuming what God is doing and allow history to test our assumptions. It is not at all unlikely that we will recognize God at work in a circumstance only when we get beyond the circumstance and view it from a historical perspective.

For those of us who have struggled with this, I'm saying that God has a tendency to hide himself from us in our present. That's what faith and hope are all about—to live our present based on knowing that God is there and that he cares deeply. The fact is that the more honest and soul-searching we become—even as we confess our doubts and fears—the more we become like the great heroes of the Bible—like Abraham, Moses, Peter, and Paul. God was very active in the present tense of their lives, but our great Bible heroes weren't always so convinced at the time. We enjoy their working faith with twenty/twenty hindsight.

Many times we discover God in our pain, confusion, disillusionment, anger—all the things that have gone on in our lives. A fellow called me recently and said, "For the last nine months I've really been going through a hard time. My career is all messed up. I don't know what's happening. I got together with another man who's going through the same thing and we decided that once a week, just out of the pain and confusion that we're feeling, we'll pull together a group of people who are also between jobs and unemployed." They've begun a fellowship group to help each other find God in the midst of these circumstances in which their careers have come to a halt. What a great opportunity! God doesn't always use just the great triumphant moments. Often he uses the pain and suffering as well.

So, how do I live my life today in the light of these facts? That's part of the revelation aspect of what Paul was praying for for the

Ephesian church, that we'd begin to see our circumstances not just through our own eyes, but with a heavenly, eternal perspective.

A Middle Eastern proverb says, "The same fire that melts the butter hardens the egg." Are we going to let what happens to us harden us or soften us to life? That's a big question. If we are to be softened we will allow the Holy Spirit to work on the "inner" person. If we are to be hardened we will look outside ourselves and blame events and persons for how our life has gone. We need to have a Holy Spirit paradigm shift. Paul tells the Ephesians that their paradigm (model) for life is allowing God to bring an eternal perspective to life by the Holy Spirit.

Seeing God in the experiences of our lives frees us from having to repeatedly play the old "tapes" to ourselves; it permits us to move on and become growing, "in-process" people. You see, unless we allow the Holy Spirit to show us that God has been with us in the midst of life and that God is working in us, then we're prone to repeat an endless negative cycle.

Perhaps you are like me. Maybe you have had some rough events in your life. I recommend that you take the time to pray and access God's grace. Reflect on the events of your life and allow the Holy Spirit to reinterpret the past for you. Bringing God to our past helps clear the path for a hopeful future and a powerful present.

Psychologists have long told us that our interpretation of events dramatically affects our behavior. In fact, an equation of $A + B = C$ has been developed. "A" stands for an activating event. Something takes place. "B" is a belief system we use to interpret the event. "C" is the consequences or resultant behavior from the combination of an event and a belief system. We're hard people to figure out in some ways. In other ways, we're as simple as $A + B = C$.

What we can learn from this psychological equation is that our belief system has everything to do with how we act. This is where faith and real life meet. It is a critical junction. If I am driven by beliefs based upon guilt, shame, low self-esteem, anger, hatred, or prejudice (the list goes on), then my behavior will reflect those erroneous beliefs in many if not all critical situations.

Do you remember the movie *On Golden Pond?* It's a classic A + B = C for me. How well I relate to Chelsea (Jane Fonda). She talks about the fact that she is grown up, lives on her own, has a great job and the respect of her co-workers, but that when she comes home she's just the fat little girl who could never dive off the board the right way. The old tapes play. Some of us feel that we are never released from our past—never allowed to grow up.

The only way to get free, move on, grow, and not play those tapes is to allow God to reinterpret the data.

I am convinced, as I said at the conclusion of chapter 2, that spiritual growth is a product of the combination of increased knowledge of self and increased knowledge of God. Growth like this moves us toward the freedom God desires for us and simultaneously moves us away from the effects of guilt, shame, anger, resentment, and other debilitating emotions.

A genuine, whole-person faith is exciting because it is bordered on every side by a loving God. There is nowhere you can run that you don't find God at work.

For instance, a whole-person faith is a faith in the future, a faith that we live a life of hope. Paul said, in essence, "I pray that this faith that I'm looking for in you Ephesians is a faith that understands that we are called to hope." Hope is one of the outworkings that Paul talks about here. It's great to know we have possibilities. Hope is something that probably fifty percent of the people in our world struggle with and lack. You can define hope this way: hope is progress toward an attainable goal. It's believing that there's something worth living for, and that you're on your way toward it.

Worry, anxiety, and fear are the enemies of hope. Each represents a dread of the future. Each is based upon an A + B = C equation in which the belief system supposes that whatever is terrible and out of control "out there" can and will take place in any given circumstance. Each tiny activating event becomes a potentially dreaded consequence because worry, anxiety, and fear occupy our belief system. They take the place of a relationship with God at the center or our lives. Hope is a future application of faith, invented by God himself to take the place of those three emotional stooges: worry, anxiety, and fear. Hope is simple yet profound. It is best learned from kids.

A child on a train trip with his mother asked when they could see his dad. The mother responded, "Tomorrow—after it gets dark and light again." Not long after this conversation, the train entered a tunnel. When it emerged on the other end, the child asked, "Is it tomorrow yet?" That is the essence of hope. Hope is believing that life is full of meaning—that change is just around the bend! Hope sees God right in the middle of the future.

I remember the movie *La Bamba,* about early rock musician Richie Valens. In the movie, Richie was petrified by a dream that he was going to die in a plane crash (which was, ironically, how he actually did die) because as a child a friend of his was killed when a plane crashed in the school playground. Richie wasn't at school that day and missed the tragedy, but for the rest of his life he repeatedly woke up with this horrifying nightmare that he was engulfed in flames and falling out of the sky. His hope for the future was very distracted because of this awful fear. This is a grim picture—yet many of us live hopelessly because we cannot imagine God being in the future.

For many of us the future is bound by the past. When we live tied to our past we are constantly drawn away from a center for living based upon a relationship with God and drawn toward an off-center belief system. Tragically, that off-center belief system based upon the past, even though it might feel safe, inevitably causes us to atrophy spiritually and emotionally.

Some of us live with a "*La Bamba*" picture for our lives. We feel that we're going nowhere, we're going down in flames. When we think these sorts of thoughts we are really painting a hopeless picture—a picture without God in it. Instead of living in hope, we choose to live in worry, anxiety, and fear.

It's been said that the two greatest fears in the world are the fear of living and the fear of dying. Either can so occupy us that we cannot function powerfully in our daily lives. Fear is the enemy of life. Hope extinguishes fear, worry, and anxiety and sets us free to live.

Paul is praying that the Ephesians and every believer will realize that God is at work in his or her life and that he's never going to quit working. He's always drawing us on to a positive goal that goes far beyond this life and anything that we could ever attain here. It includes eternity with him, with the One who made us.

This eternal nature of hope became clear to me when I was visiting with a man who runs a halfway house for problem teenagers. Most of them have been physically and sexually abused. Very few have a prognosis for what we would call a normal life. In the midst of all the despair, the halfway house director has hope for the kids. He told me, "For a lot of these folks it must be like it was for the thief on the cross next to Jesus. I can almost hear Jesus saying, 'No, you haven't amounted to much in this world, but today you will be with me in paradise.'"

Hope has no end. Some people are so hurt, so beaten, so damaged by this world that if hope were limited to this life alone, they could not expect any. But some of us whose bodies, minds, or emotions are permanently damaged can still have hope. Even though we have been crushed by experiences and left so immobilized by life's hurts that there is not time enough in life to fix those hurts, we can still have hope—hope for relief in the eternal life that God promises us in Jesus Christ. Hope begins on planet Earth and extends into life eternal.

Beyond hope Paul prays for a whole-person faith that knows that we're clear of the past. He prays that you would know your "inheritance" as a child of God.

Several years ago, one of my friends had a terrible experience. His father was a fine Christian leader in the community and was one of my heroes and a dear friend. Definitely someone wise, he was a person that I would turn to for advice.

One day, my friend got a call from a relative saying that his dad, who had suffered a series of nervous breakdowns and was emotionally weakened, had walked down to the garage with a shotgun and taken his own life.

My friend was devastated. All of us who knew his father were in deep shock. My buddy took a job in another town to clear his mind out. He was haunted for two or three years by fears that the way he was brought up and how much he was like his father were going to lead him to commit suicide too. That horrible thing that happened to his father made him crippled by his own past. Statistics might bear out that fear. But what makes hope in Christ significant is that we can live beyond the statistics.

One day, my friend had an emotional experience in which he realized that he had an inheritance. He was a child of God. He wasn't just Barb and Bob's kid; he was God's kid! And God isn't dead. He's still alive. God never committed suicide. My friend realized that he was adopted as a son of God and was free from his past.

Now maybe some of us haven't come to grips with that in terms of our past, but it's the truth. You're God's kid. I'm God's kid. We don't need to be tied down or have our lives determined by what's gone on in the past. In fact, we can usually walk back through the past and see God's hand in it, as I mentioned earlier.

In addition to the possibilities of a hopeful future and a past that is reconciled, you and I have potential for *now*. Whole-person faith is knowing that God is on our side. He is on our side in a way that brings power and comfort and strength to our lives and guidance to make life work each day.

At my worst, the strength to live today sometimes comes down to the fact that the sun will set and come up again tomorrow. Have you ever had a day like that? Today's rotten, but I can have the faith for today just because, thank God, it's going to end. In fact, some people are afraid to die, but I'm really glad that people live about eighty years and die. I don't want to go through this for eternity!

I'm glad that my days are numbered—that all our days are numbered. I don't want my friend who has a terrible case of cancer to suffer forever. He has a far better future in heaven beyond the insult of death and decay. He will be pain-free. I'm glad for the way that God has made the world. I am enjoying learning to live by faith.

A whole-person faith comes down to this: we are free of our past and have enough hope for the future that we can believe in God's power for now—today.

While God's overall will and direction for our lives may appear to be hidden from us, God does manifest his presence in remarkable and meaningful ways in our daily lives. We can look back at points in our lives and affirm that God's fingerprints are all over events and circumstances. The fact of God in our past drives us to the awareness that God must somehow be at work in the present and in the future.

The goal of Paul's prayer is a worthy goal for you and me: that we would strive to know God in a deeper way, in an integrated way, in a whole-person way. Because of what God has done for us and the way we know him and understand his heart and his compassion for us, we become more beneficial in the lives of others. I've seen God do it time and again in everyday people. If you are without hope today and if you're struggling, let me share with you one last story. It's the story of my friend Bill.

Bill was one of the most hopeless people that I have ever met. He was the kind of person who would wear a green shirt, brown checkered pants, a gray checkered jacket, and tan shoes. Bill was a guy who could barely talk to himself, let alone anybody else, without getting nervous. Bill scored about a minus seven on the self-confidence scale. He had a self-image that stunk. Bill worked in a professional office and about the only thing he felt comfortable doing was working at a drawing board all day long.

Bill began to pray for himself the kinds of prayers Paul prayed for the Ephesian Christians. Bill began to see God at work in his life. He prayed to have the courage to meet some people and make some friends. He met some folks and began going to a small group Bible study in our church. Suddenly, he began to feel that he was worth something. When he told his unique story and shared his deepest fears, people laughed and said, "Oh, we feel like that too!" It was great for Bill to be sitting next to an ex-college football player, talking about how he struggled and felt like a nerd and couldn't do anything right, and to have that former football player who appeared to have it all together say, "Oh yeah, me too!"

As Bill found himself accepted by this group, he began to say, "For the first time in my life, I'm going to take a chance and risk myself to do some ministry and be involved in other people's lives." He said he wanted to work with the church's high school group. He went to the high school and started to meet kids and they loved him. They would come up to Bill and talk and sit with Bill at the ball games and Bill felt pretty good about that. Kids started to say how important Bill had become in their lives. In time, Bill got very good at working with youth. It's now been about a decade and Bill's still working with kids in the same church. And that's not all . . .

He started to think, well, that's great, but no one would ever want to marry me. Then, he met a woman in the church. He had new confidence, she saw the great things that he had done in young people's lives, and her conclusion was that if he could love kids and commit himself to kids as he had, then he was a guy who could probably be committed to another person for the rest of his life.

They fell in love, they got married, they've had kids, and Bill's whole life, though still full of growth and struggle, is a testimony to God's goodness. Bill has found what we all want—a past that is purged, a future full of hope, and a powerful present experience with Christ. He is living Paul's prayer for wisdom and revelation in the 1990s.

PART
TWO

Introduction

The cross upon which Jesus Christ died to provide an antidote to the human condition of sin becomes the focal point in Ephesians 2:1–3:21. People are not made new by their extreme efforts to grow, expand, and improve, but rather they are made new by surrender.

Grace comes out of surrender. Grace is unmerited good-standing in God's presence. Grace is belonging. This foundational relationship with God is a starting point on the spiritual journey. But it is only the beginning.

Partnership with God in the "re-creation" process is our opportunity to extend grace to our world. Re-creating what? God in Christ is active in a fallen world restoring that which is dilapidated and broken. And we colabor with him in meeting the needs of a hurting and hungry world. God takes a risk working with less than perfect human beings. But as we live in Christ and work with Christ in the world, our faith experience deepens. We discover enormous change taking place in our lives, the result of God's deep work in our inner person.

4

Fully
Alive

As for you, you were dead in your transgressions
and sins, in which you used to live when you followed the ways of this world and of the ruler of
the kingdom of the air, the spirit who is now at
work in those who are disobedient. All of us also
lived among them at one time, gratifying the
cravings of our sinful nature and following its
desires and thoughts. Like the rest, we were by
nature objects of wrath. But because of his great
love for us, God, who is rich in mercy, made us
alive with Christ even when we were dead in
transgressions—it is by grace you have been
saved. And God raised us up with Christ and
seated us with him in the heavenly realms in
Christ Jesus, in order that in the coming ages he
might show the incomparable riches of his
grace, expressed in his kindness to us in Christ
Jesus. For it is by grace you have been saved,
through faith—and this not from yourselves, it
is the gift of God—not by works, so that no one
can boast. For we are God's workmanship, created in Christ Jesus to do good works, which
God prepared in advance for us to do.

EPHESIANS 2:1-10

My wife, Nancy, likes a room on the cool side. I like it warm. One day we got into one of those silly marital disputes to which many of us can relate. It was a fight over room temperature. I just wouldn't back off. A small squabble turned into a full-scale war. Our voices became louder and louder. I can still remember the scene in our kitchen. I was holding a glass of water. At the crescendo of our argument I sent my glass crashing to the floor in pieces and stormed out of the house for a long walk (in the cold I was trying to escape earlier). I remember my emotions well. I felt dead. Deep inside I felt like a hopeless, useless, dead "thing."

Experiences like this remind me of my humanity. There really is an off-center force in me that is self-destructive. It is a force representing decay, death, and any other word descriptive of unwholeness. It's called sin. It's a force to be reckoned with. And God has a plan.

The introduction to the second chapter of Ephesians is a marvelous piece of scripture. It tells us all about who we are and what we are like at the core—and it tells us all about who God is and what he is like at the heart. It is a picture of decrepit human beings made valuable as the miracle of God's love is poured out upon human beings like you and me.

We have all joked about the word *sin* and referred to someone who was breaking one of the social mores at the office as a "sinner," but I am convinced that we really do not like to talk about or seriously entertain the idea of sin. What is sin? Am I a sinner? Yet, all of us can point to an experience like my glass-shattering fight and acknowledge an out-of-control portion of our person. Somehow though, we feel that if we admit we are imperfect, everything will break down. We fear that our self-esteem will erode and that we'll see ourselves as wormish, useless people.

Most of us want to live under the illusion that we are good people and deny that there are destructive forces at work inside of us. We fear that if we admit to the presence of those dark forces, they will somehow take over or we will be humiliated to a point of collapse. Yet, it is the very act of admitting those dark forces and surrendering to a higher power, known as the Holy Spirit, that ultimately sets us free.

Sin is a tough word. It points to shortcomings and failure. None of us likes that. Sin exposes a side of us that we don't want to reckon with even in our most isolated alone-time, let alone affirm in public. Yet, the biblical story of the human race is very clear about the fact that we human beings have made choices and continue to make choices that are at cross-purposes with the God who created us and claims control of this world.

I learned a lesson about being at cross-purposes from the game of golf. I am not a good golfer, but I enjoy hitting the ball around the course as often as possible. At one point a few years ago I was ready to quit the game. I was working intensely on my swing, trying to hit the ball straighter. I had taken lessons and read volumes of golf advice on how to fix my swing. Each time I approached the ball, I would recite all this golf advice to myself, tighten into one giant body spasm, and whack the ball anywhere but where I intended it to go. If you are a golfer, you can relate to this.

I was trying to focus on too many things at once. What I needed was to surrender to the swing that I had practiced and free myself to hit the ball by thinking of just one thing. Releasing my wrists as a part of the swing was the biggest lesson I had learned, so I told myself "let the wrists go" and then swung. My "let the wrists go" cue freed me from all other distractions and I began hitting the ball pretty well. This revelation about golf has done a lot to help me in the rest of life. When I become defensive about my shortcomings and then become overly focused on fixing myself and being a good person and doing things "my way," I go into a sort of spiritual spasm caused by self-reliance. The heart of sin is pride and self-reliance.

This may be old news to you, but I'd like to take a moment to define the word *sin*. The ancient Greek word for sin is *hamartia* (hah-mar-tee-uh). It is a military word used in target practice. A first-century target was a distant mark. When someone doing target practice blew it, the range master would yell "*Hamartia*," meaning "You missed the mark." That is the source of the word we call sin today. Sin is missing the mark—shooting with perhaps the best intent, but failing to score a bull's-eye.

The Scriptures relate much of the story of woman and man from creation clear to the generation or two after Jesus Christ lived on earth. The story of humankind is marked by a keen recognition that we have missed that mark. We have failed to live as God intends. Our failure to do so is sin. Sin has rendered us useless as far as finding true meaning and fulfillment in life. Sin throws us off center.

My dad owned a machine shop. I got to go there a fair bit as a kid. I remember a story that one of the machinists told me a long time ago. It had to do with a grinding wheel. As you probably know, grinding wheels turn on a shaft at very high speed. They need to be balanced around the center. The machinist told me the story of a wheel that got seriously "out of round" when a machinist was using it. The unbalanced spin eventually caused the wheel to come apart. It exploded into dangerous fragments that flew all over the shop. The grinding wheel couldn't withstand the force of spinning off center. Neither can we. We explode spiritually, emotionally, and socially when we lose our center.

In Ephesians, the apostle Paul describes human beings as "dead." In one sense, this could mean empty and useless. On the other hand, it can describe the end of a process wherein some of us have been devoured by our own lusts, compulsions, and obsessions, our twisted values and our willingness to obey the voice of Evil rather than obey God. I think that Paul's description of spiritual death is a compilation of any or all of these things. He describes human beings as being so hard toward God and his ways that they become by nature enemies of God.

Thank goodness our friend Paul doesn't sign off leaving us with just the bad news. He goes on to write about the God who is rich— so very wealthy with an overabundance of love—and filled with mercy. God pities the messes that we have made of ourselves. He reaches down to us and pulls us out of our mess. Kenneth Filkins has caught this beautifully in a poem, which I have edited slightly, entitled "The Pit":

A man fell into a pit and he couldn't get out.

A SUBJECTIVE PERSON came along and said:
"I feel for you down there."

An OBJECTIVE PERSON came along and said:
"It's logical that someone would fall down there."

A CHRISTIAN SCIENTIST came along and said:
"You only think that you are in the pit."

A CHARISMATIC TRIUMPHALIST came along and said:
"Just confess you are not in the pit."

A PHARISEE said:
"Only a bad person would fall in a pit."

A FUNDAMENTALIST said:
"You deserve your pit."

BUDDHA said:
"Your pit is only a state of mind."

A HINDU said:
"This pit is for purging you and making you more perfect."

CONFUCIUS said:
"If you would have listened to me, you would never have fallen into that pit."

A NEW AGER said:
"Maybe you should network with some other pit dwellers."

An EVOLUTIONIST said:
"You are a rejected mutant destined to be removed from the evolutionary cycle. You are going to die in the pit so you do not produce inferior pit-falling offspring."

A SELF-PITYING PERSON said:
"You haven't seen anything until you've seen my pit."

A NEWS REPORTER said:
"Could I have the exclusive story on your pit?"

An I.R.S. MAN said:
"Have you paid your taxes on that pit?"

A COUNTY INSPECTOR said:
>   "Do you have a permit for that pit?"

A REALIST said:
>   "That's a pit."

An IDEALIST said:
>   "The world shouldn't have pits."

An OPTIMIST said:
>   "Things could be worse."

A PESSIMIST said:
>   "Things will get worse."

JESUS, SEEING THE MAN, TOOK HIM BY THE HAND AND LIFTED HIM OUT OF THE PIT.

Jesus Christ has lifted us out of the pit. That's the good news. *Even though we were dead in sins and trespasses, we are made alive together with Christ Jesus.* We have been rescued by the grace of God, who has simply chosen to have mercy upon us and pull us out of the pit when we call for help. No rationalizations, no requirements, no help from us—just mercy from God. This great act of love by God is referred to in Scripture as the New Covenant.

I remember sitting in one of my first theology classes when my professor and now dear friend, Dr. Michael Mates, said, "The only requirement for inclusion into the New Covenant is that you be a complete failure." He went on to quote from Hebrews (8:8), which says, "And finding fault with them, God said, I shall establish a new covenant."

Most of us would like to come to God with the idea that we deserve fresh, new, fulfilling, life-changing, all-renewing power to live a new life because of some deed we have accomplished. We would remind God of the old lady whose lawn we mowed, the handicapped person we fed by hand at the state institution, or the way we have nurtured family members. But that won't work as a ticket.

God's requirement, his only requirement—the sole ticket to New Life—is admission of failure.

So, fully alive in Christ begins where we end. New life begins when we come to grips with the fact that in spite of all our practice, we miss the target of God's plan for life. In our admission of failure we gain admission to God's family, and the adventure of life lived to the maximum begins. The adventure of new life is not without its problems, however.

Even as my fingers push the keys on my computer to write this chapter, I am aware that some of us who claim to be God's children don't feel all that alive. We don't feel all that free from the ways of this world, from the negative impulses of our human nature, or from our self-centered values. I often still feel imprisoned by those things. The problem is a gap between what I know is possible somewhere "out there" and the nearness of my current predicaments.

I really know what I can be in Christ—but I want it all now—and when I fall short of the ideal, I condemn myself severely. I tend to cast myself back in the pit and wallow in it. I have a tendency to jump in and take control of things, thinking that God has somehow disappeared. I inevitably make things worse.

I remember the time I cut someone off in traffic completely by accident and the other driver became very hostile. I rolled down my window and sincerely apologized. The person began berating me. At that point I got mad and told him off. It felt good for about two seconds, then I was overtaken by an emptiness inside that gave way to depression. Not only did I feel bad about cutting the other driver off, I felt bad about striking back verbally; then I felt bad about feeling bad. The whole thing turned into a downward spiral of self-doubt and self-hatred. It was out of control. I lost all perspective and was depressed for two or three hours.

If you are like me, you can relate to that sort of self-condemnation. In a way, it's good. We don't want to settle for anything but the best and our failures frustrate us. But we also ruin life for ourselves and those around us when we live in the pit.

I call this problem the perception gap. We fall back on habits very easily, and for some reason most of us are pretty well programmed to the negative. So even though we have come to Christ and become his disciples and know the possibilities for our lives, we still relate best to our predicament of being dead in sin. We have a new center for life, but it doesn't always seem to have the power we need. Therefore, when we fail, we refer back to our predicament of feeling totally lost and out of it rather than experiencing the mercy of God and moving ahead. The perception gap. We revert to an old state of affairs rather than living the new life we are given. Recently, I have been trying something new . . . and let me tell you it has taken a real conscious effort. When I struggle, I can face one of two directions. I can do as I am accustomed to doing and look behind me to my predicament—to my pit. Or I can look ahead of me to my possibilities—and to Christ who has rescued me. I have been striving to remember to look ahead. I am learning when I struggle to say, "Lord Jesus, you have already forgiven me for my shortcomings. I accept that. I know that you made me and that you know me and love me—but I am struggling. I feel like a loser. Help me find a way to look ahead to what I am becoming instead of being caught up in the inadequacies of who I am."

My old friend and former colleague in ministry, Brad Henning, is a man of many insights. I will never forget what he said about this issue of letting go of what is behind (for the majority of us, that is a huge quantity of guilt and shame) and looking ahead to what is new. Brad demonstrated his approach to a group of us by saying, "Close your eyes and think of the ugliest, most awful red-faced monkey that you can envision. Memorize its features and face." He waited a few moments in silence and then said, "Now, I don't want you to think about red-faced monkeys at all for the next five minutes. Okay. Starting now, don't think about that awful monkey at all. No thinking about red-faced monkeys."

Well, we all got the point. What a good illustration of what focusing on an object can do to us. It colors all that we think about in the future. If we focus on our failures, our guilt and shame, then we are paralyzed by them. We must choose where to focus. We either focus upon the new center for living—faith in Jesus Christ—or we center on our old habits. We are free to choose.

Thank goodness that God in his love for us doesn't want us to haul around the baggage of our failures with us. He forgives us for our sins and sets us free to have a fresh start. That is not just a one-time experience but a daily reality.

When we fail and our conscience goes off like a smoke alarm and we are filled with noxious fumes of guilt and shame over our shortcomings, we can come to God in Christ and simply confess our failure. At that point we are forgiven and cleansed with an on-rushing torrent of new life and new beginnings.

Too often, I place my personal sense of worth in how I perform. If I'm a good guy one day, I am valuable. If I struggle or fall short, I am garbage. What many of us need to learn is that our value is not based upon what we do but rather on who we are, and who we belong to. We are of great value because God said so. The remarkable thing about the love of God is that it doesn't come into the world seeking that which is valuable. Rather, God's love pours into the world to make each of us valuable. He loves us. In his mercy, God has come down into our pit and rescued us. He has said, "You are worth it—believe it—you are of great value. Don't fear, because I am with you."

God places extreme value on you and me. Every time I read the story that C. S. Lewis tells in *Miracles* about the greatest miracle of all—the miracle of God coming to rescue us—I am astounded.

> In the Christian story, God descends to re-ascend. He comes down; down from the heights of absolute being into time and space, down into humanity; down even still if embryologists are right, to recapitulate in the womb ancient and pre-human phases of life; down the very roots and sea-bed of the nature he created. But he goes down to come up again and bring the whole ruined world with him. . . . one may think of a diver first reducing himself to nakedness, then glancing in mid-air, then gone with a splash, vanished, running down and through green and warm

water into black and cold water, down through increasing pressure to the deathlike region of ooze and slime and old decay; then up again, back to colour and light, his lungs almost bursting, till suddenly he breaks surface again, holding in his hand the dripping, precious thing that he went down to recover. He and it are both coloured now that they have come up into the light; down below where it lay colorless in the dark, he lost his colour too.

Through the whole process of "becoming like us" Christ demonstrated his ability to identify with us where we are. He did so in order for us to become like him. The end of this amazing passage in Ephesians 2 says that when we are made alive in Christ, the fact is affirmed that "we are God's workmanship, created in Christ Jesus for good works, which God prepared in advance for us to do."

The great good news is that Christ has given us the true freedom to live in the joy of being nothing but our absolute best. We are freed up from the past. Free to live today and tomorrow with purpose, with direction, with the very strength of God within us.

We won't always succeed, but we have the freedom to succeed— and the grace of God to forgive us and put us back on the track when we do not.

When Pope John Paul, the leader of the largest Christian denomination, spoke in Atlanta on a recent visit to the United States, he referred to the freedom we have in Christ by saying, "True freedom implies that we are capable of choosing good without restraint." He said this is the kind of freedom we should seek rather than acting as if we are only free "when rejecting every objective norm of conduct, refusing to assume responsibility, or even refusing to put curbs on instincts and passions."

We become truly free when we let go of our predicaments and shortcomings and our need to cover up for being less than perfect and accept the fact that we belong to God and that he has great plans for us.

You can dream dreams with God and do great things in partnership with God. Let go of your predicaments and grab onto the possibilities of being fully alive in Christ—possibilities that are perhaps best summed up in the words of this old hymn:

Take my life and let it be, consecrated Lord to thee.
Take my moments and my days, let them flow in ceaseless praise.
Take my hands and let them move at the impulse of your love.
Take my feet and let them be swift and beautiful for thee.
Take my will and make it thine, it shall be no longer mine.
Take my heart it is thine own, it shall be thy royal throne.

Our great admission of failure and our great response to God's love by surrender empowers us to begin living life the way God has planned, with him at the center of our lives working his grace and forgiveness in us from the inside out.

As we live and breathe the reality of this new life, we begin to strike out into the world, looking for our place to belong with confidence. We can know that God is with us. We can trust him and begin to love others with the knowledge that God is about the same business in their lives too. More about that as we move on.

5 Cornerstone

Therefore, remember that formerly you who are Gentiles by birth and called "uncircumcised" by those who call themselves "the circumcision" (that done in the body by the hands of men)—remember that at that time you were separate from Christ, excluded from citizenship in Israel and foreigners to the covenants of the promise, without hope and without God in the world. But now in Christ Jesus you who once were far away have been brought near through the blood of Christ. For he himself is our peace, who has made the two one and has destroyed the barrier, the dividing wall of hostility, by abolishing in his flesh the law with its commandments and regulations. His purpose was to create in himself one new man out of the two, thus making peace, and in this one body to reconcile both of them to God through the cross, by which he put to death their hostility. He came and preached peace to you who were far away and peace to those who were near. For through him we both have access to the Father by one Spirit. Consequently, you are no longer foreigners and aliens, but fellow citizens with God's people and members of God's household, built on the foundation of the apostles and prophets, with Christ Jesus himself as the chief cornerstone. In him the whole building is joined together and rises to become a holy temple in the Lord. And in him you too are being built together to become a dwelling in which God lives by his Spirit.

EPHESIANS 2:11-22

I have often tried to categorize the best and worst years of my life. The best years were certainly those in which I had great successes—my relationships were exciting, like the year Nancy gave birth to our daughter, Rachel. I also remember bad years characterized by no progress in my career and by failed relationships. The good years seemed to flow with meaning and purpose. I seemed to belong. In the bad years, I was a stranger living inside my own body.

I can think of no worse year than the seventh grade. Do you remember seventh grade? That's the year that you want to die. Seventh grade was the year I watched a story unfold that I always dreaded might become my story.

A new kid had moved to our neighborhood. I will call him Fred. He was in my seventh-grade physical education class taught by Mr. Zurfluh, who we called Mr. Zee. Mr. Zee practiced a custom many of us are familiar with. Each Friday we had a physical fitness test. It took the entire hour. It was humiliating to anyone who wasn't at least of average size, strength, and coordination.

We went through all the stations to test running, jumping, strength, and endurance. The last test was the rope climb. I was a big kid and Mr. Zee would always look at me and say, "Rowland, give the rope a break." I did some push-ups and lots of sit-ups, but I took a zero on the rope. I took the job of holding the rope to stabilize it for the others to climb on. Fred, the new kid, needed a few extra points to make a good showing since he had just moved into town. He didn't know anyone and no one knew him. He started to climb the rope. Halfway up, Fred fainted.

Mr. Zee hollered, "Look out, everybody!" Fred came down on the mats, out cold. Six years later when we graduated from high school there were jeers and chuckles for "Fred the Fainter" as he went to grab his diploma. On that day in seventh grade, he was brand new to the school. He didn't know anybody. One thing happened in his life and it became a symbol of his failure and inadequacy. The rest of his school days were lived as "Fred the Fainter." Fred didn't belong.

I had a similar experience in fourth and fifth grades. My mother would stand in front of the picture window of our house and look across the road at the Tacoma City Light station. It had a side lawn shaped like a narrow football field. She would watch little Randy in fourth grade with his helmet and pads go over and play football with kids who were in sixth or seventh grade. I really wanted to be like the older kids.

They did horrible things to me. For instance, they would say, "Randy, you get to run with the ball this time." They'd say it loud enough for the defensive huddle to hear. Then all the guys would tackle me; even the guys on my own team would jump on me. The seventh graders would grab my face mask and drag me around. Every day I would cry. They would say, "Stop crying," and I would say, "I'm not crying, I just got dirt in my eyes when nineteen of you jumped on me."

I'd come home crying, and my mother would say, "Don't go play football." I had to go play football because it was too important to belong, no matter what happened to me. So I continued to get my brains beat in daily.

I think all of us have experiences of being included or being excluded etched on our memories. Belonging is something that we deeply yearn for and we'll do just about anything to look like we belong.

Ephesians offers us one of the greatest glimpses of belonging that I have ever seen. The need to belong is at the heart of so many of our anxieties and struggles. The need to belong is at the heart of so many things that all of us do wrong that mess up our lives. In other words, by seeking to belong we choose inappropriate channels and we wind up in ruins. "Fred the Fainter" actually failed by trying too hard to belong. I failed with the neighborhood kids because I felt I just had to play football, even if I was much younger than the rest of the gang.

Paul begins this passage by discussing the distinction between Jews and Gentiles. This was a great controversy in the first century because the Jews believed that the promise of the gospel, the Messiah, belonged to them. No one else could believe in Jesus unless they first became like the Jews and followed Jewish tradition.

I opened this chapter talking about the woes of being a seventh grader. Isn't this like the seventh-grade mentality? Fit in perfectly right now or you'll be a reject forever. Paul addresses this problem by saying that Jesus Christ has spoken "peace to you who were far away and peace to those who were near."

The Gentiles said that Jesus had taken them by surprise. They claimed that he was the Lord who forgives sins and makes lives meaningful just as he had done with the Jews. They wanted to know, "Do we have to become Jews to enjoy this?" There was a big division.

Along came the apostle Paul. He was preaching to the Gentiles. Paul actually got into a battle with some other apostles about the right of Gentiles to belong to Jesus Christ without having to become Jews first. They all met in Jerusalem and finally decided that Christianity could work without conforming to Jewish culture. Whether a person fits in or seems a million miles out of it, Jesus Christ is here to accept that person.

The issue is not innovation versus tradition or anything else. It is a battle to distinguish who and what is worthy of giving us our identity and sense of significance. Paul argues vehemently that it is no more and no less than our relationship with Christ that gives us worth. God is in the business of making both those who think they have it all together and those who think they are worthless vital members of his family.

As this section of Ephesians continues, Paul declares that until Christ entered the world, we were all without hope and excluded from God's promised plans for the universe. Hope and promise. These two key words merit exploration.

It is interesting to note, as you read the Old Testament, that God made a lot of promises, and most of the promises included the same things. They included the fact that the people who followed God would become a big family. They also would have a unique influence in the world, and, finally, they would have a special relationship with God. Paul is saying that because everyone who belongs to Christ belongs to God, God's promises to all generations are for those who belong to Christ.

God's promise to take a diverse group of people and make them one loving family is for everyone who belongs to Christ, irrespective of culture and other qualifications. I belong. That's important to me. Further, God promises that he will use his family to work out his plans for a world of hope, healing, justice, and peace. I want to be involved in meaningful activity. On top of that, God promises his presence to those who follow him. We can know God personally.

What Paul is saying is that when we understand that we belong in this world, our new identity brings us to a place of hope. Remember, hope is best defined as making progress toward a discernible goal. As we understand that we belong, we are set free to see a future full of possibilities. Those possibilities include intimacy and acceptance in the family of God, meaningful engagement with the world around us, and the warmth of an intimate relationship with God. When we recognize that we belong, we begin to see that we matter—that our lives make a difference.

Part of the special relationship with God that we are promised enables us to communicate with God openly about who we are and what we are facing. Paul says that we "have access to the Father by one Spirit." "Access" in Greek is *prosagogane,* and it means "permission to approach a king." In Jewish tradition the Jews were special people and God was their king. The Jews were the ones who had the right to approach the king; no one else did. Paul is making the outrageous statement that everybody has the right to approach the king. There is no nobility in God's family!

Paul further emphasizes the equal standing we all have in God's eyes by saying that we are "no longer foreigners and aliens, but fellow citizens with God's people." Foreigners and aliens were those who lived in the Jewish city-state but had no rights. They lived, worked, and paid taxes there but had no right to say anything about what was going on. This old order is countermanded by Paul's argument that we are all "one" in God's family, and that because we are one, we are committed to the inclusion of all sorts of people in God's family.

That process of including all people in God's family is what Paul refers to when he says, "You too are being built together." In construction terms, being built together means "framed." The framing process is the part that gives shape and strength to a structure. Our diverse personalities, gifts, and styles are a source of pleasing shape and a component of strength in the building of the Body of Christ.

The final verses of Ephesians 2 precede a very practical section of the letter. I really think that Paul is warming us up for the meat of what God has been teaching him about a relevant Christian life. And I am convinced that he did not feel that he could move on in his letter until he discussed the source of our identity.

All of us yearn to belong. Yet sometimes, in our own sense of incompleteness, we attempt wild ways of establishing our identity. We run looking for love and acceptance in all the wrong places. When we go somewhere other than to our Creator for our identity we miss the mark. We are off target. As I discussed earlier, the Greek word for "sin" means to miss the target.

Sin has two effects. First, when I am alienated from God and out of sync with my Creator, I get out of sync with myself and I cannot have peace. When I am in that state I cannot have an internal psychological sense of serenity. Second, when self-alienation sets in, we begin having problems with the others in our world. We project our own shortcomings onto people and institutions around us. We begin to have problems dealing with those in our world. For instance, my insecurity over belonging causes me to place high expectations on my family—I insist that they communicate how important I am. I can easily accuse them of not being close-knit enough. And yet my yearning to belong at all costs actually results in alienation.

How often I have wondered about the life of "Fred the Fainter." Would he have made it to the top of the rope if he had felt accepted? If he felt okay about himself and free to succeed or fail in front of his peers, would he have been propelled to get the extra points he needed in that PE class? Or, conversely, could we have seen his exhaustion and simply freed him up to not have to try the climb?

I wonder about my football adventures on the City Light lot. Maybe I could have been allowed to belong as a younger participant and encouraged rather than pommeled.

Many years have passed now. And, as I understand this section of Ephesians, the only thing that can avert my tendency to look for all the wrong ways to belong is a personal relationship with Jesus Christ. Jesus' death on the cross and subsequent resurrection give him the power to empower me. Jesus' presence in the center of my life by way of the Holy Spirit conquers the alienation I fear and dread. The presence of Jesus offers belonging.

The apostle Paul is consumed with the centrality of Christ for all of life. He declares that Christ is absolutely central. He announces that God's plan for the world is built "with Jesus Christ himself as the chief cornerstone." God is building a new kind of family—a group of people who belong to him. Jesus Christ is the eldest sibling, the oldest heir—the cornerstone.

If you understand construction, then you know Paul is saying that Jesus is the central focus of all that God is doing in the world. Jesus is the most important supporting member of God's building plan, the main source of alignment for the structure. Further, Christ is the key reference point. Instead of being floating planks in a sea of despair, we are connected to the Cornerstone and given definition and purpose. His strength becomes our strength. His alignment and direction become our alignment and direction. His purpose for being becomes our purpose for being.

The cross is a symbol of the cost of belonging. That gruesome symbol reminds me that God went to great lengths to say to me that I am important to him. God paid the price for us to belong. The cross snaps us to our senses. It reminds us of what Christ did to make us belong. It reminds me that Christ says we do belong to him and to God's family.

The good news is that if you feel far away from God, he is still right there fighting for you. If you think you are real cozy with God and you don't feel that you need him (except on Sundays because you are an achiever), the good news is still the same for you. You need Jesus Christ to put the pieces of your life together, and he is ready to do it.

Another important lesson is taught here in Ephesians. It flows from our sense of belonging. Jesus calls us fellow citizens and sets us free to include others. Whom do you treat like a stranger and an alien? Are you homophobic? Do you have a lack of respect for blue-collar workers or people who are less intelligent than you and your peers? How do you treat people who are dressed differently? Are you a sexist? What about religious styles? Personality styles? Habits? We all have the tendency to treat other people as strangers and aliens, but in Christ the barriers and dividing walls are broken down and we are made one.

If we are going to be a part of God's plan, then we are going to be framed end to end with people who may be offensive to us. Jesus Christ is framing the Church. We don't have a choice about where we fit in and to whom we are connected. We are an unlikely bunch built together by God to reach out and love the world. Belonging is critical to all of us, but what we do when we consider others as strangers and aliens is to create a system that says, "Here is what I am willing to belong to, and here are the ones I won't belong to." In Christ, we don't have that choice. We're family. And you don't get to pick your siblings.

Perhaps I have some relatives who weird me out, absolutely. They make me furiously mad, and I think they are as strange as all get-out. But you know what? We have the same last name. You can do anything to avoid the weirdos, but when you have the same last name, there is nothing you can do about it. As part of God's family we all bear the name of Christ, our Lord. We need to turn ourselves to Christ and open ourselves to a wide diversity of people. This is very condemning to me. We need to take the chance to let God do something beautiful.

6 Risky Business

For this reason I, Paul, the prisoner of Christ Jesus for the sake of you Gentiles—Surely you have heard about the administration of God's grace that was given to me for you, that is, the mystery made known to me by revelation, as I have already written briefly. In reading this, then, you will be able to understand my insight into the mystery of Christ, which was not made known to men in other generations as it has now been revealed by the Spirit to God's holy apostles and prophets. This mystery is that through the gospel the Gentiles are heirs together with Israel, members together of one body, and sharers together in the promise in Christ Jesus. I became a servant of this gospel by the gift of God's grace given me through the working of his power. Although I am less than the least of all God's people, this grace was given me: to preach to the Gentiles the unsearchable riches of Christ, and to make plain to everyone the administration of this mystery, which for ages past was kept hidden in God, who created all things. His intent was that now, through the church, the manifold wisdom of God should be made known to the rulers and authorities in the heavenly realms, according to his eternal purpose which he accomplished in Christ Jesus our Lord. In him and through faith in him we may approach God with freedom and confidence. I ask you, therefore, not to be discouraged because of my sufferings for you, which are your glory.

EPHESIANS 3:1-13

My parents went to Hawaii when I was in the eleventh grade. They left my great-aunt with us children. She was over seventy years old. Aunt Laura had a good head, but she couldn't handle the business of the house. So before he and Mom left, Dad wrote out all the bills that would need to be paid during the three-week trip and also made out deposit slips for his paychecks. I was supposed to sign his name, mail in the paychecks to the bank on the appropriate days, and mail all the bills on the days they were due.

Well, I was more into peace, love, and Woodstock than bank deposits and bill paying, so I wasn't overly attentive. Somehow the check deposit slips and bills all got knocked off the desk in my dad's work area and wound up on the floor. Out of sight, out of mind. At the end of the three weeks, just before my folks returned, I remembered the bills but forgot the paycheck deposits from Dad's business. I mailed all the bills out but never deposited the checks. My parents came back to a string of bounced checks. My dad wanted to murder me, but he settled for making it one of those adolescent object lessons.

The second chance taken on me also happened when I was in high school. There was a brand new teacher in school. Mr. Goin was fresh out of college and still wet behind the ears. One day as I walked by him he said "hi." When I responded, he said, "Come over here." I said, "I didn't do anything!" He told me that he liked my voice, and that I should be in drama. In fact, he was holding tryouts for *Blithe Spirit* by Noël Coward. I had never been in a play, but I auditioned well. I got the lead role. I had never memorized anything more demanding than Led Zeppelin lyrics. In fact, I had just memorized my name and address when I was sixteen, and my life-style in the sixties was threatening to erase that.

Two and a half weeks before the play was to go on, Mr. Goin canned me from the part and replaced me with someone else, because I couldn't remember all the lines. Mr. Goin took a chance on me, and I blew it.

I think of those experiences when I read Ephesians 3:1–13. I call it "risky business." Do you remember the movie *Risky Business*? A boy's parents leave for vacation and their son runs an illicit escort service out of the house. The teenager closes the operation and puts the house back together just as his parents return home. The morals of the business were clearly out of line, but what an example of pushing risk to the limits.

I need to review a little bit in order to set up where we will be going in this chapter. What I've seen and what I've been describing to you from Ephesians is a matrix for making life work. Paul, imprisoned in Rome near the end of his life, is looking back at his experience of life and faith and putting everything into perspective. He concludes that what God has in mind is that our past can be redeemed, traded in for something new and useful, and that our lives can be filled with hope. Redemption from the past means giving all that is behind us in our lives a new meaning. The past is actually reinterpreted by our present experience of God's grace. When our past is put together in the right way, and our future is perceived in the right way, we find ourselves in a "now" that really works.

Hope is a sense of progress toward a positive goal. While we become free from or actually empowered by our past, God gently but steadily pulls us toward the future. We need to have a future that is built with hope, but we need to ground our hope in the present.

If I told you that you were going to die in twenty-four hours, you probably wouldn't do very much planning for the future as far as your finances are concerned. But if I told you that in thirty days you would inherit a million dollars from a relative you never knew who had passed away, you would probably take some of your spare time and begin to ask, "Where do I invest this money? How do I use this inheritance to take care of my needs and the needs of those I love?"

When we have a hope that is grounded in the present, we begin doing things now that really count. We invest in the inheritance we have received as children of God. This is something that the people of the 1990s really struggle with. We have a tendency to walk through the world like ghosts. We can walk through walls, we can walk through circumstances, we can walk through people as if we are invisible and insubstantial, because we have not understood how to get free of our past, lock into our hope, and begin to exercise our newfound freedom with positive, productive steps in our present.

We tend to live by excuses: "If that hadn't happened to me I'd be a more complete person," or "When this and that thing changes in my life I'm going to get on track." We slip through our present experiences missing a lot of days that could really count. We are looking for "pie in the sky." We deny ourselves into nonexistence. We would-a, could-a, should-a, and if-only our way into a semi-comatose state and then say that's all life has to offer.

While we are busy telling ourselves that our past has ruined us, that our future is bleak, and that our present situation is untenable, God is in the business of jerking us to our senses and setting us up in a franchised partnership with himself as meaning makers, people builders, and world changers. God bets on us. He takes the ultimate risk of calling us his partners in the midst of reclaiming our lives from the trash pile. God enters into a risky business! He beckons us to life on the high wire as part of his show.

God puts people in risky places. It is in the risky places that our characters can develop and our gifts emerge. Because of the incident with my dad, I have an almost obsessive desire not to pay a bill late. And because you'll recall my earlier story about not having enough money to pay bills, you can see how much it drove me crazy not to be able to make ends meet. I'm organized, I leave everything in a special place. This has almost become a fault for me and it drives my significant others mad. I learned from that experience and new gifts have emerged. In ten years as a radio announcer I never went on the air without a clear idea of what that day's show was about. I learned that from not being ready to play the lead in the high school play from which I was canned. You might say that my failures in past stressful and risky situations became fertilizer to help me grow. I have developed new attitudes and new behaviors.

These have equipped me for new and even more stressful and risky situations.

In the same way that living in relationship with God puts us in risky situations, we put God at risk, because we claim his name as his children in the world. It seems to me that he is saddled with the greatest of liabilities, given what people are like. Think of the shame and liability that the parents in the movie *Risky Business* faced. God takes a risk with us. God could have said, "I'm going to blot out all the unrighteous ones and keep all the good ones." He could have flown over the earth in a blimp and announced what he is all about and what people should do.

Instead, God became a human being. He was challenged with all the ups and downs of life, just as we are. In the person of Jesus Christ, God walked the earth for thirty-three years. His whole business was to take on twelve clowns that would make even the best leadership trainer faint. These were twelve common people with all the common hang-ups. They were insecure, power-hungry, disloyal, lying, stealing folks just like you and me. Jesus simply hung around with them. He told them that the world was in their hands and that they would pass the baton of God's grace through the generations.

Some people believe that God comes to us in his grace and puts up with our shenanigans. I doubt that they would allow for the fact that God takes risks with us. But God does take a tremendous risk by investing himself in us and calling us partners in his plan for the world. Some people won't like the fact that I have said this. Yet, I am sure that God does take risks.

God takes a risk in allowing me to be called his follower. What do I mean by this? In situations where God needs his love or concern shown, he at times entrusts you or me to do that loving or caring. Sometimes we do well. At other times we fail. We come up way short and God has to use another plan. God is ultimately God and can cover our mistakes—therefore his plan is ultimately accomplished, but he still takes a risk in the here and now. I like this idea. You and I, as people who belong to God, are his plan.

Certainly God has a plan for history, but even more significant is the fact that he has a plan for developing people. God is in the people business. He designs us, directs us, and empowers us to be his grace transmitters, if you will allow the "techno" term.

Being followers of Christ also puts us at risk. Sometimes we take chances that appear to be good moves at the start. The apostle Paul was in a tight spot, under arrest. He said to his captors, "I am a Roman citizen, I appeal to Caesar." Had he not said that, he might have gotten out of jail with his skin on and walked away.

Instead, he ended up under arrest in Rome and never left. He eventually was executed at the hands of the rulers to whom he had appealed for help. Paul wound up in jail for making the move he thought was right. I don't think we need to glorify how much he liked being in prison. It wasn't all that great a situation, but Paul learned how to make it count. In a strange way, God even allowed a bad risk to pay off.

A few years ago my interest in working with high school students in a youth group put me in conflict with my boss at a radio station where I had a really good job. My boss thought I was being too openly religious. Eventually, the conflict forced me to resign my job and start a private business . . . which failed. When we follow God, it doesn't mean that everything works out great. Sometimes there is a downside to things. We fail. We learn. Taking risks really develops character. Paul's time in jail gave him confidence that God could work through anything. My own pain in life has proved to be a gift. I too have begun to learn that God can be there for me in the ups and downs of this crazy life. I am learning that in the midst of both my greatest failures and my greatest successes, God can use me to help build his eternal kingdom.

I don't want to blow smoke at you if you are hurting. I've been there. I know what it is like to be in a bad spot and feel that life isn't going very well. But I do want you to know that wherever you are, you can be used by God. I think this is something that we really need to understand. So many of us feel that we have to become eloquent, educated, socially acceptable. We believe we have to have our lives together. Some of us have a list of things, written or unwritten, that we feel we have to do before God can use us. The good news is that none of that is true. God can take you and use you wherever you are right now!

Let's come back to the idea of the "now." We won't easily let ourselves be connected to "now." It's scary to live in the present. We feel hung out to dry having to stake all of who we are and all we hope to be on today. That's a bit silly, though, because the past has already happened and we can't do anything about it. The future is uncertain. We can be dreamers and think about the future, which is fine, but that doesn't really help us today. The place where we are on the line, and at risk, is in the present. That is why so many of us are afraid to engage in it. The worst stress to endure is the stress of having to deal with the present.

It is the stress of living in the here and now that brings out new gifts and qualities in us. Sometimes we are in the toughest of places, perhaps a job that we hate, or a relationship that is eating us alive, and we have to endure the time between our realization that we are suffering and the resolution of that suffering. Some of the greatest pieces of our character will be put together in those long and painful interludes in life. We have to listen to the pain and bring our pain to God as a spiritual discipline. Pain is an unavoidable part of life. There is never a place this side of eternity where pain goes away—there are only attempts to deny or drown pain. Those attempts account for much of the trouble we get into and much of the emotional sickness so many of us suffer.

Keep in mind that Paul wrote to the Ephesians from prison. I think we all have prisons of our own that make us feel trapped or locked up. How about bad jobs, bad memories, mental illness, alcohol or drug dependencies, sexual struggles, grief, disappointment, too much success, too much or too little money, too many responsibilities? The question that I have is, Do you have or will you develop a confidence in God that says he can make a difference in those situations? I'm not a foxhole Christian who, when things go bad, says, "Oh God, if you help me now I'll be better." I'm the kind of person who has a solid faith and a great relationship with God when life is going well. When things get lousy, though, I switch into a survival mode. Randy takes over and I run the show myself. What I am learning is to say to God in the midst of the bad times, "I really need you."

Dire circumstances also bring out the real "us." I know that when I am under pressure, my tendency is to be short-tempered, to take control, to want the world to revolve around me, to jump right to the front. It is at our very worst that we recognize our need to change and grow—and it is also at our very worst that we forge the elements of character that change us as people.

I know of a parent, Janice, whose oldest child was killed in a tragic accident just as Barbara was reaching adulthood. The situation was devastating. As Janice came upon those gathered at the scene of the fatal accident, a remarkable event took place. This loving parent, obviously taken with grief, went to the young people involved in the accident and assured them that they were not to blame. Right there, Janice prayed that none of the people who were on the scene would be troubled by guilt. She also prayed for the rescue team looking for Barbara's body.

In an astounding way, this well-centered follower of Christ took a leadership role at the scene of a terrible event, making decisions and taking actions that would forever transform those who were on the scene. Indeed, God invests himself in us and then asks us to risk the act of faith when we are in tough spots. If we take the risk, we become leaders. The rewards can be great.

Leadership and risk are related. Risk is at the heart of leadership. European Communists in the 1960s had a slogan, "Every Communist a leader, every leader a Communist." Their wish was that everybody who was a Communist would become a leader, and they dreamed that every person who had a leadership role would become a Communist. I hold a similar view as a Christian. I feel that every Christian should be an influence maker, a servant-leader, creating influence wherever she or he is. "Every Christian a leader and every leader a Christian."

True leadership is not appointed, it is recognized. A lot of us are walking around saying, "I'd like to lead something, I'm waiting for someone to call." That isn't how it works. You hang your fanny out, you take some chances, you put your life on the line, you serve some people, and you try to make a difference. An old Chinese proverb goes like this: "If you say you are a leader and no one follows, you are just out for a walk." When people eventually start to follow and move in the direction you're going, then you are a leader. It's risky. You have to tell your story and share your failures before leadership begins to happen. Leadership is recognized. "Who is already doing it?"

In Ephesians 3:10–11 Paul indicates that God's manifold wisdom is revealed through the church. This is also what I mean by risky business. If I were God I wouldn't take flawed instruments (human beings) and put them in charge of a delicate and often misguided institution (the church) and then choose to direct all the wisdom and knowledge I have through this one mouthpiece on earth. It would be too risky for me to handle.

Let's look at that phrase, "manifold wisdom." The word *manifold* refers to the way that a diamond is cut with many facets. The image Paul is creating here is of a church in which we learn to embrace and encourage each other with our different qualities and styles. It is a big step of spiritual maturity not only to acknowledge different styles, but to have the confidence to join with those who are different, to go out into the world and show a sparkle from all the different sides of God's personality to all the different facets of this world.

Some of us are emotional in how we express ourselves, yet we are going to be the reflective light of God's love to people in the world who need a lot of emotional support. Others may say, "I'm on the intellectual side, and I am a good friend to those who operate intellectually." One characteristic of a diamond's facets is that they don't face each other. So we all stand back to back reflecting out to the world God's glory and his manifold wisdom, and that's part of God's plan. We get into trouble when we try to force everyone to think and behave the same. When we get caught up in the comparison game, we wind up turning our own strengths into weaknesses and denying the power that comes through diversity. The comparison game always leaves us feeling arrogant or inadequate. Neither of these is particularly useful.

If God can unite the diverse weirdos in the church, then he has got to be all-powerful. I'm acquainted with a famous Christian speaker with whom I strongly disagree about ninety percent of the time. I'm sure he doesn't often agree with me either. I can argue about his theology, I can talk about his methods and styles, and even about the fact that I think he makes people feel guilty. But the bottom line is, I cannot argue with the guy's spirit. I have to love him. I see the fruit of what he has done. I see that he is sincere. I see that he has made great sacrifices to do what he does. I could argue with everything else, but I can't argue with the fact that the spirit of God is within this man. Part of God's plan in uniting us is to blow the world away, so that such a diverse group of people can like each other and even work together for a common cause.

Perhaps you remember the movie *Tucker*. It's the story of a man who fought the Detroit automobile industry attempting to introduce a car named after himself. In one scene, Tucker is talking about how his mother came from the old country. She was Italian and had a very heavy accent. Tucker remembered that for years when he was young she said to him, "Don't get too close to people, you'll catch their dreams." What she was really saying in broken English was, "Don't get too close to people, you'll catch their germs." But Tucker grew up thinking, "Don't get too close to people or you'll catch their dreams." I think that what Tucker thought he heard his mother say was closer to the heart of human fears than the fear of getting the flu. When we get together in a group and talk about our passions, we catch each other's dreams.

It is frightening to tell of our greatest dreams, because we are afraid they might not come true and others will know. Also, we don't want the responsibility of having empowered the dreams of others. All of this is frightening. It feels way too risky. We tend to fear that others may succeed while we fail. Plus, if I get close to you and catch your dream, I have to jump in with you or support you, and that is risky business. Yet I am overwhelmingly convinced that one of the beauties of being God's people is a chance to brush shoulders and catch each other's dreams. That's where we really begin to discover God's dreams for this world—when we open up and hear each other and allow a diverse "big picture" to emerge.

I love high school kids. High school was the greatest time in my life. I have always been interested in teenagers. Perhaps that's what has led me to stay in touch with a remarkable organization called Young Life. It all began with a dream. Sometime around World War II, a guy named Jim Rayburn came out of seminary, and he didn't like the way kids were being treated in the church. He didn't think they were getting biblical content or growing in faith. He pulled a group of kids together and started meeting with them. He called these gatherings Young Life.

Now, over fifty years later, Young Life has spanned the globe because people got next to Jim Rayburn's dream—and they caught it. I can name organization after organization where people have come together and caught each other's dreams and done great things for God. I'm saying, Get next to each other. You may catch a few germs, but you will also catch some dreams.

People want to be connected with God and other people. In Ephesians 3, Paul captures the heart of that desire and all the risk that it involves both on God's part and on our part. It's good news that God risks his reputation with us. It's good that we have the opportunity to risk our lives with him. Keep these things in mind:

1. God is the God of love. He identifies with us intensely. He made us. He became one of us. He is fully aware of the risk he takes investing in flawed human beings and he delights in it.

2. God is the God who sustains us. This is where the power of the Holy Spirit comes in. As God sends us out into the meat of

life, as we encounter new challenges and risks, God's Spirit gives us the resources of strength, wisdom, encouragement, and endurance to help us succeed.

3. God empowers us with gifts. We are actually equipped by God to do his work in the world. He miraculously uses us in every-day situations.

4. God is a God who will never leave us. Frankly, I've been a bad boy most of my life. But in the midst of this rebellion, God has been with me. And I've learned that there is no way God will ever dump on me or ever leave me.

5. God allows us constant access to him. We are welcome to come into God's presence to vent our fears, concerns, and needs. Or we can simply come to him to get refreshed. We need to take more advantage of that access.

6. God expects us to have confidence. Confidence does not mean cockiness. It means knowing absolutely that God is for us. It means I live with a certainty that God will always provide what I need—not necessarily what I want—in every situation in life. If I have confidence, I can know that God will take care of me because he loves me.

7

From the Inside Out

For this reason I kneel before the Father, from
whom his whole family in heaven and on earth
derives its name. I pray that out of his glorious
riches he may strengthen you with power
through his Spirit in your inner being, so that
Christ may dwell in your hearts through faith.
And I pray that you, being rooted and established in love, may have power, together with all
the saints, to grasp how wide and long and high
and deep is the love of Christ, and to know this
love that surpasses knowledge—that you may be
filled to the measure of all the fullness of God.

EPHESIANS 3:14-19

Physicists keep looking for the unifying principle that holds
the world together. So far, they are stuck. They see many of
the pieces of what makes this world tick, but they are unable
to find the core element or unifying principle. Scientists are searching for the glue—the life force—that holds the world together.

Paul believes that he has discovered that force. He believes that
God, from whom every atom—every family—derives its name, is
behind it all.

Albert Einstein, one of the great physicists of our time, was once
asked what his goal in research was. "I want to know God's
thoughts, " he said. "Everything else is details." Einstein had the

same understanding of the universe as Paul. In fact, he once said, "Religion without science is lame, but science without religion is blind." Einstein was well aware of the fact that God is the unifying principle behind the very physics of the universe. Paul understands that it is God who is holding the world together despite the disastrous damage introduced into the universe by the human family. Sin has shaken the structure of all that is. Decay is everywhere. The world appears to be falling apart—and we seem focused on the symptoms, not the actual problems.

In light of the state of things, Paul appeals to the God who is working in Christ to pull creation back together. He is praying for the emergence of a New Creation. He prays for God to reassemble things. He prays that the reassembly might begin at a very deep level.

God begins work at the core of every believer—in her or his innermost being. God is thinking long-term. He desires for us stability and permanent transformations. God works in each of our lives from the inside out. That means that deep belief and attitudinal changes take place before anything is ever seen on the outside by anyone else.

Paul was familiar with Greek thought about virtues. The virtues compelled persons to call upon their own inner power. The power was possessed by human beings and simply needed to be accessed. The virtues called for an exercise of willpower to create good behavior.

Paul was also familiar with mystery religions. Some had to do with sex-goddess worship or bizarre bloodletting rites. These mystery religions claimed that the gods could be manipulated or controlled by human incantations. A puff of smoke and a loud shout and a god would be at their beck and call.

In the midst of a first-century culture that was not altogether different from our own, Paul pleads to God that Christians be empowered—from the inside out—by the Holy Spirit. Again, we see that Christians are to be new creations, not built with human power but re-created (there's that re-creation word again) by the power of the Holy Spirit.

Paul understood what we need to understand: If this world is going to change and be saved from ruin, it is going to be changed by the Holy Spirit–empowered followers of Christ. It will not be changed by magical mystery tours into trippy spiritualities that depend upon crystals, codes, and rituals. It will not be a world changed by human willpower. It will not even be changed by human goodness.

If you read some of Paul's other letters, such as Galatians, you will see that there is another blocker to God's re-creation. It is not humanism or some sort of New Age mysticism. Rather, it is religiosity. Religion is dead and cannot offer new life. The world will not be changed by self-sacrificing, self-disciplined religious people who operate on willpower.

Religion operates on preset systems that assume God's presence but are not dependent upon his support. For example, there are Christian discipleship programs abounding that can be purchased in book, cassette, or video format—or one can go to a seminar and get the input up close and personal. Now, not all discipleship programs are bad, but some are. In fact, they're awful. What they attempt to do is take the outgrowth of what the Holy Spirit works in believers' lives from the inside out and impose that upon persons externally.

Religiosity decides what the authentic fruit of discipleship looks like, then describes it as actions that can be learned. Some Christian leaders focus on behaviors that have been labeled "Christian." They miss the fact that what makes one truly Christian is the presence of Christ at the center of one's life. Adherence to mere behaviors is some people's definition of godliness. For these leaders, godliness can be taught as a behavior.

To some, godliness looks like abstaining from certain social habits such as dancing, listening or not listening to certain types of music, and never swearing. These may indeed be godly behaviors, but one does not need God's Spirit within to do them or to abstain from doing them. I know many persons who object to dancing because it takes place in loud crowds. I know others who shun rock music because they think it is trash. And I know many a person who never curses, holding to Will Rogers's notion that people swear only because they don't have the brains to come up with anything else to say. All these behaviors may be moral and good and right. God may even lead us to such choices. But these behaviors are not in and of themselves godly. Godliness is a result of being in communion with God. It is not the result of adhering to a list of behaviors that please some denomination or sect.

Religion seeks to replicate the fruit of God's work in one's life without God. Paul, in another of his letters, refers to this as "having a form of godliness but denying its power." (2 Tim. 3:5).

In compulsive-behavior groups that deal with drug, food, alcohol, and sexual addiction, people discover that willpower and human determination and self-help are like throwing coals on a fire. The exertion of will actually enables the dysfunction. What needs to happen is surrender. Surrender indicates that something is going on in the depths of the personality. It means that we who surrender are allowing ourselves to, in the electrician's term, be rewired. It's the opposite of instinct. We want to be militant toward the aspects of ourselves and our lives that nag at us. We want to exercise control. Yet it is our controlling behavior that has allowed us to paint ourselves into a corner to begin with.

In Twelve-Step groups that treat compulsive behavior, one of the early steps toward recovery is an admission that one has a need for a Higher Power—that the individual is totally helpless in finding recovery on her or his own power. What a great place to come to in our faith journey as well. After all, isn't the struggle we face rooted in the fact that we are compulsive sinners, that our very nature is to miss the mark, to misfire our emotions, our motives, our behavior—all resulting in strings of messes we leave for God or someone else to clean up.

We learn all too often how empty our faith is. One of the things I am continually finding is that God will not allow me to be complacent. The faith style I had five years ago doesn't work any longer. When I resort to ritual and try to pull out tapes from my faith journey that are five years old, they won't play. I am left empty, anxious, scrambling. Then, in desperation, I surrender—usually after attempting all alternatives. I surrender and let God be God—and I retire from the position for a while.

Our Christianity is many times as ritualistic and dependent upon "magical cures" and "incantations" as our former First Lady's pursuit of astrology. We laugh that the wife of a United States president who claims to be Christian would use an astrologer to set meeting dates for her husband, but if we take a hard look at our own faith, it sometimes looks just about as juvenile. If you don't believe that, consider the Christian leader who claimed that God would kill him if his followers didn't donate enough money to his ministry.

The magic approach and the stoic willpower approach to faith have at least two things in common. First, they both deny the power of God by his Holy Spirit. They pour the water of human folly on the fire of God that seeks to renew each of us. Second, each of these approaches to religion is externally focused. So often we believe that manipulation of external objects, events, or environments is capable of enabling internal change. This is simply not so. You will generally find that content and well-adjusted people are content and well adjusted in most circumstances. They have developed inner qualities that make life work.

Gordon MacDonald, in his book *Ordering Your Private World,* describes what he calls the sinkhole syndrome. Sinkholes are those gigantic areas of instability underlying the surface of the ground. After a period of time and under the weight of the external environment, the ground caves in to reveal a deep, gaping hole. Everything on the surface is sucked beneath and destroyed.

This happens often as a natural phenomenon in areas like south Florida—and it happens a lot as a spiritual phenomenon in places like Seattle, San Francisco, Denver, New York, Chicago, St. Louis, and Grand Rapids as many of us place the tremendous weight of modern life upon a flimsy emotional and spiritual superstructure. We constantly cave in.

Pascal said that there is a God-shaped vacuum in the heart of every man and woman. We all desire to be filled to the maximum with God—to sense in our deepest person his love and affirmation. We desire to know rationally and experience at an existential level a love so significant that we feel grounded—held together.

What does that sort of grounding look like?

It means acknowledging a need for Christ, allowing him to be central in our lives. This only sounds easy. First of all, let me explain what I don't mean. I don't mean to imply here that we can have perfectly pure motives and be perfectly centered people. All of us are in some way damaged goods. I need to look at my life and myself honestly. Our lives flow in a basic direction, like a river. Rivers have eddies that flow sideways or even backwards in relation to the basic direction, but there is a predominant course. We must courageously examine the direction of our lives. Are we flowing toward Christ? Or are we moving toward self-determination?

It means being open and vulnerable to others about our deepest needs. I still remember that day several years ago when I felt that I was a complete stranger to myself and everyone else—including some dear friends and my wife, Nancy, who is my best friend. I was desperate to talk with Nancy. I picked her up at home and we drove to a marina near our house and pointed the car into a parking stall facing the water. I broke down in tears and said, "Honey, I need you." That was the first time I had ever spoken those words to any human being. Rather than saying, "Why?" or better, "Why didn't you realize this sooner?" Nancy just held me while I bawled. I was set free to allow God to use others in my life.

The next day I went to a meeting with a group of four men with whom I have met weekly for five or six years to pray and share. I told them that I had always been honest in telling my story and sharing my needs, concerns, and struggles, but that I had never told them before that I needed them. I let them know, as I let Nancy know, that I had come to the end of my rope of self-sufficiency. It was scary to let go, but I have been a changed person since.

It means building our sense of value (self-worth) and significance on the fact that we are children of God. It is getting to be a well-worn assertion in Christian circles that our sense of identity comes from being children of God. We do pay it lip service. But the truth is that until we learn that the only audience we have to play to is God, we will never be truly whole persons. My dear friend John Westfall and I were talking recently. John is an insightful and prophetic person—and usually does folks the favor of telling them the truth. Well, as we were chatting, I told him that I don't really desire to be a number-one guy in any organization, not in business or as a pastor. He said he knew that. I said that the reason is that I am not really a strong leader. He disagreed. He said, "You are a strong leader. You have the skills to be the number-one guy in many big places, but your personal insecurity and fear of rejection won't allow you to be on the point. It is not a matter of skills; it is a matter of where you choose to go to find your sense of value and self-worth." I went home with his words ringing in my ears. Westfall is right. I am in process.

It means acknowledging others as unique creations of God. I once supervised a person who was very competent, without peer in her field. But she had no idea how to treat people. She was forever looking over her glasses at others when they didn't comprehend her strategy and saying, "Aren't you smart enough to get this?" Or, when asked for help, she would simply tell someone, "That's not important to me. Do it yourself." She might even end such a conversation by just placing the telephone in the cradle and hanging up.

We had some tough conversations about the value of people. Slowly, she began responding and now is able to train others to do the same excellent work that she does herself. I think she is blossoming into a people lover. She has caught God's vision.

My friend's new behavior comes as an act of surrender. It is the act of declaring God to be the one who works in lives, not us. Too often we behave like the discipleship programs I discussed earlier

in this chapter. We come to those around us who are wounded, in
need, in progress—just like us—and we cover them with a huge
pile of expectations for their behavior. We play God and give others their ten commandments. God doesn't need apprentices; he
doesn't need fill-ins, because he is not planning vacation anytime
soon. And he surely doesn't need someone applying for his job,
which, for the span of eternity, is already taken.

It is living our lives from the inside out. Imagine the freedom to
live without performing for strokes from others. Image the freedom to build brick by brick the way that God directs you rather
than being tied to the religious expectations of others. Recently I
was chatting with a man over dinner. Three years ago, he was
homeless. A drifter. A bona fide alcoholic. A person who had failed
in two marriages. For the past three years, he has been on a faith
adventure with Jesus Christ. God is transforming him from the
inside out. He has his own successful business. He will be remar-
ried soon. He has a home. God is doing a great miracle.

As this man pulled a pack of cigarettes out of his pocket to go
stand on the deck and have a smoke (since the house we were in
was a no-smoking zone), he said, "I guess God will get after these
soon and I'll be able to quit smoking." He continued, "It probably
won't be as hard as settling down or drying out."

I wanted to stand up and cheer. God was working from the inside out for this new friend of mine. He acknowledged that God
hadn't finished his work on him by a long shot. He knew smoking
was a poor choice—but he was too busy cooperating with God on
the repair of some other bad choices he had made to even worry
about it yet.

*It is living above our circumstances, realizing that true peace comes
from internal change.* I once saw a picture of a tiny bird in a tree.
The tree hung on the very edge of a river in a raging storm; it
looked like it was ready to topple. But the baby bird didn't even notice. The title of this picture was *Peace.*

I cannot claim to experience that kind of peace. Most of my
friends would tell you that I am a proficient worrier, and that even

though I tend toward optimism, I can really get blue sometimes in the midst of negative circumstances. But it is in these circumstances that you and I can discover the true meaning of peace. Negative circumstances can be God's way of moving us along in life. Recently I sat with a young friend whose job had gone sour on him. He was depressed by the way he was being treated at work. He was obviously being forced out by a boss who didn't like his style. As I prayed for my friend Mark, I said, "God, I don't for a minute pray that Mark will thank you for what he is going through now. That wouldn't be right. You don't necessarily engineer our difficult times just to see how we'll do. But I do pray that Mark will be able to thank you for the character, understanding, and wisdom you built in him through this experience when he is further down the road from it."

I am not a prophet. But I do believe there is truth in that prayer. Our tough times shape us. They bring change. They bring new levels of faith and tenacity. Tough times plus God's resources in the center of our being forever change the way we walk through life.

PART
THREE

Introduction

I struggle to make my inner and outer lives congruent with one another.

The baby boomers have been the source of much study by those who write about Christian spirituality and Christian ethics. We seem to be a very spiritual generation, but when it comes to aligning belief and behavior we have some real problems. Recent surveys show that while over twenty-five percent of the baby-boomer population claims to have a personal faith in Christ, over half that number relies solely on "personal experience" to make life's decisions. Personal ethics and life-styles are the place where Scripture and baby boomers run into real difficulties. Yet, it is clear that God calls us to consider a new life-style as we move deeper in our relationship with Jesus Christ.

Personal change may occur from the inside of the individual and move toward outward action, but the fact is that if outwardly transformed behavior, behavior that aligns itself with scriptural principles, never happens, there is a profound problem. Such a failure in bearing fruit would indicate a systemic problem in a fruit-bearing tree. So it is with spirituality. If our spirituality is not bearing fruit, it is an indication of a systemic spiritual problem, an indication that a true connection and communion with Christ is not being achieved. This does not mean that we are ever going to be perfect or holy persons. Such a belief in perfectionism is an age-old falsity. But what Ephesians 4:1–5:20 does indicate is that God's work deep within our lives is evidenced by external change as a response to God's transforming grace.

I believe I remember the concept of "cases" from English classes dating back to junior high school. The indicative case is descriptive of action. Another case is the imperative, which demands action. As I read Paul's letter to the Ephesians, it is clear to me that we must have our cases straight. Chapters 1–3 are in the imperative. There is an action demanded of us. The demand is that you and I be "in Christ." Chapters 4–6 are indicative. They describe the action that flows from Christ-centered lives.

People who have experienced the imperative of grace are people who are in process or "under construction." Part 3 of this book deals with some of the indicatives, the signposts or channel markers of a Christian life-style.

8   The Walk of Life

> As a prisoner for the Lord, then, I urge you to
> live a life worthy of the calling you have received.
> Be completely humble and gentle; be patient,
> bearing with one another in love. Make every ef-
> fort to keep the unity of the Spirit through the
> bond of peace. There is one body and one
> Spirit—just as you were called to one hope
> when you were called—one Lord, one faith, one
> baptism; one God and Father of all, who is over
> all and through all and in all.
>
> EPHESIANS 4:1-6

I recently picked up the Saturday morning paper and found a small article describing a new product on the market. The product is the Boss-Tear-Apart-Stress Doll. The article documents advertisements for the doll that read, "Because its appendages are attached by Velcro, you can rip the head, arms, and legs right off this beady-eyed captain of industry." Priced at a scant $19.95, this innovative product expresses the philosophy held by many of us. It says that we are right to justify our own goodness, be it at work or anywhere else, and then rip to shreds those who are in our way or don't please us.

The apostle Paul offers a glimpse of how God dreams our relationships could be. I think if Paul had been selling a Velcro-jointed doll, it would have been shipped in pieces, with the object being to put it back together again. In the midst of the brokenness of our world, Paul envisioned a manner of walking through life that is constructive rather than destructive—a walk that values others and nurtures relationships. This represents a radically new personal style for most of us.

Why do we so frequently find ourselves wanting the doll with detachable body parts so that we can ritualistically disassemble others? I think it is because we tend to get caught up in the moments of life and fail to have a greater perspective, a perspective that life is a long haul. We think short-term. We experience our own personal needs profoundly and we expect those needs to be met immediately, perpetually, and by all who surround us. Such an attitude of entitlement is not conducive to long-term health either personally or interpersonally.

A French proverb says, "You not only have to want what you want, but you have to want what your want leads to." This is a thought-provoking idea. It says that to really get the most out of life, we need to take a long-term perspective. As I struggle with chronic overweight, this proverb haunts me at every food table in a social gathering. I want the hors d'oeuvre, it tastes great—but do I want what my want leads to? Perhaps you have struggled with a chronic disease. I was recently diagnosed diabetic. I have become acutely aware of the fact that satisfying my immediate wants could bring an early and miserable end to my life here on earth. Most of our self-destructive and ungodly behavior is a result of myopia—the inability to see beyond what is right in front of us.

The frightening thing about our behavior is that, as Christians, God gives us the freedom to choose good or bad, better or best, life or death at any turn. Even when our wants are short-sighted, we often get them anyway. Psalm 106:15 is a shocker! "So God gave them what they asked for, but sent a wasting disease upon them." Imagine that. God is patient enough to give us what we want—to let us have our way—but it may result in a very nonfulfilling spiritual and emotional state. Psalm 106 was written by King David, a known adulterer and murderer. He exercised violence to satisfy a moment of lust when he saw a beautiful woman bathing on the roof of a neighboring house. He enters into an adulterous relationship with the woman and arranges to have her husband killed in battle. It's a horrifying story of runaway instant gratification and short-term thinking. His selfish, short-sighted relational wants led to extreme leanness in his life. It nearly cost David everything.

Nowhere in life does our decision—the walk we choose—manifest itself more clearly than in the quality of our relationships. The walk of life is the walk of significant and meaningful relationships. The walk of life has a source; it has signs and a specific shape. I want to take a look at those. The source of the walk of life is found in the apostle Paul's invitation to respond to the grace that God has extended to each of us. God empowers us. I don't want to overuse the word *empower,* but it is a key to so much of how Paul understands God's relationship with his forever family. Notice in this passage that Paul asks followers of Christ to walk in a manner "worthy of the calling you have received." Good grief. At first blush, that sounds like guilt-inducing stuff. But I did a little research into the Greek and the word *worthy* has its roots in the language of scales and measurements. It means to create equivalence, literally to "bring up the other beam of the scale."

Imagine that. God acts first and places the weight of his love and forgiveness on a plate at one beam on the scale. To respond properly means to balance out the other side in acknowledgment of what God has done for us. So, walking in a "worthy" manner isn't a demand for perfection. Rather, it's an encouragement to be responsive to God's grace—to respond in kind to the depth of experience we have found.

One day recently I was reading in the Bible about God's desire to make everyone his child. That struck me hard, because I sort of want God to clear people with me before he admits them into his eternal kingdom. I really felt moved by the fact that God has rescued me from myself and my destructive tendencies. I felt an urge inside me to "balance the scale." So I committed to pray for the well-being of the next people I saw who struck me as odd. Bad prayer. I got up from my desk and walked less than one hundred yards before I wound up in the middle of a Psychic Fair in the lobby of our office building. People were huddled around tables reading palms, checking vibrations, telling the future from cards, and looking at crystal balls.

My immediate response would have been to become judgmental. But the voice of the Holy Spirit down inside me spoke stronger than my prejudices. I began praying for each of the folks at the psychic fair. I thanked God that they were seekers who were not willing to live life just at the material level. I praised God for their spiritual sensitivity. I began to pray that God would bless each of those people with fulfillment in life—first and foremost by guiding their spiritual journeys eventually to him.

I was shocked at myself. I actually responded to the grace God had invested in me. I experienced new life—a real transforming event. I did it out of relationship with God—not out of obligation to be a "good guy."

Responding freely to God takes us off the performance bandwagon and out of the traps of guilt and shame. This allows us to risk ourselves by responding to Ultimate Love with our own offering of love. The whole walk of life flows from this concept: that the source of the walk of life is love freely given and that the walk is love freely returned—love toward God and love toward our fellow human beings.

We move a step deeper into Paul's discussion of the walk of life. We come to the "signs" of the walk. There appear to be five signs of the walk of life in this text. They have to do with a response to grace involving personal attitudes and adjustments that facilitate good relationships. I find Paul's list challenging—far beyond my resources, even far beyond my own desires.

Sign number one is humility. Humility is not groveling wimpiness. Rather, it is viewing and valuing oneself for who one is in the sight of God. The Greek word for humility was a slave term referring to "absolute servility." It was a word that described persons who possessed no rights and claimed no identity. Imagine that. If we treated all of life as a gift from God, we would live it without an attitude of entitlement.

The renowned Oxford scholar C. S. Lewis wrote a book called *The Great Divorce.* It is a story of persons on a bus leaving Hell and going for a day's visit to Heaven. During the trip, one man confronts the bus driver and demands information—he says that he "demands his rights." He is told by the driver that if he will just sit down and be quiet he will get far better than he deserves.

That is the essence of humility, to accept life and relationships as a gift of grace. So many of us are busy demanding our rights and liberating ourselves—to what end we may not know—that we wind up getting far less out of life than is intended. We demand what we deserve—and wind up getting it. The fact is, God desires to give us better than we deserve.

Claiming no identity is the other side of humility. Some studies I have read of the adult population in America say that one of the great psychological illnesses of our time is "image monitoring." Image monitoring is the act of always looking for clues and seeking feedback from others as to how we are projecting ourselves and then adjusting our behavior to fulfill the image we want to project. This is a self-defeating behavior that denies the uniqueness of each person's character and instead creates a false persona.

Do you remember the movie *Zelig,* in which Woody Allen, one of the true latter-day prophets, plays a character who physically becomes like whoever he is around? If he hangs out with Asian friends, his features become Asian. Likewise, when he spends time with doctors, he becomes one. This character suffered from a loss of identity that catapulted him into a pathological state of image monitoring. Humility is a state of accepting who we are—warts, wiggles, curves, and all.

Sign number two of the walk of life is gentleness. Gentleness is strength that knows who it is. It's John Wayne and Clint Eastwood without the macho. Gentleness is assertiveness through genuine concern for others. One of the early church fathers, Bernard of Clairvaux, said, "Learn that if you are to do the work of a prophet what you need is not a scepter, but a hoe." Gentleness channels our strength of character in a serving and nurturing direction and away from a ruling, legislating, or strangling posture in relationships.

I have to tell you about a friend of mine. His name is Charle Young. Charle was an all-American football player, an NFL first-round draft pick, and a big star in pro football. He is about six-foot-seven and weighs over 250 pounds. He is a marvelous Christian who will shake your hand and make it disappear in his huge palm. On the field he was tough mentally and physically. Off the field, he possesses the same strength of character. It has made him a lifetime success. And you don't ever hear Charle being intimidating. That giant of a man has the gift of gentleness as he stands next to others with his encouragement and advice.

Sign number three of the walk of life is long-suffering. Long-suffering is not a word that exists in our modern conversation. It is derived from an ancient Hebrew word describing God's "steadfast love." It denotes a quality beyond patience. It is patience in action. It means being forbearing of others. The word *forbearing* is also a little off the beaten path from most of our language in the 1990s. But what forbearing basically means is putting up with something in someone else that you know you can't change. What an unbearable thought. Yet, long-suffering is one quality that develops in us as a response to God's putting up with our endless string of shenanigans.

Long-suffering also includes in its meaning "withholding justice." Long-suffering means that we don't retaliate even when it is deserved. I will never forget one of my great failures in the long-suffering department—a true face-first stumble on the walk of life.

One afternoon a business associate and I went to look at a certain make of imported automobile. My friend already owned one and I was looking around. We saw what looked like a good car from the road and drove in to check it out. After a few minutes a salesman came out to greet us. He answered several questions about the car. He could see that we had come in a car of the same make.

When I requested a test-drive, the salesman asked me very bluntly if I was going to buy that car. I didn't know how to respond. I said I was surely interested but couldn't guarantee anything—but could I drive it anyway. He told me that if I wasn't going to buy the car, I couldn't test-drive it. Obviously, he wasn't having a good day. So, being the fine Christian I am, a purveyor of long-suffering, I asked him if he was born a jerk or had to go to college to become one. He responded that he had to study hard. I retaliated further, saying that he had clearly been successful beyond all imagination, possibly graduating magna cum laude. With my cute, quick tongue I publicly humiliated him and further added to whatever pain he must have been experiencing in his life.

I got in my friend's car, laughing at how I had hosed that jerk salesman down. Then, ever so quietly, God's spirit gently apprehended the real magna cum laude jerk and showed me how little I had put on the scale to "even it up." I had thoroughly failed to respond to the long-suffering God has shown me through the years. I felt about three inches tall. But to show you how long-suffering God is—as I confessed my sin, the Holy Spirit seemed to say to me, "The scale is even now. Your realization evens the scale for now. Continue the walk of life."

The fourth sign of the walk of life is a catchall. It is love. Love is seeking the highest good for another. Love is a consciously chosen action. Love is a proactive behavior and attitude that forcefully replaces anger, bitterness, and resentment. Paul uses love in this sense in Ephesians 4:1–6.

A lot of what love is about is a willingness to drive off the negatives in relationships. Love is a willingness to forgive. Forgiving love benefits both the lover and the loved one. On January 9, 1984, a *Time* magazine article said:

The psychological case for forgiveness is overwhelmingly persuasive. Not to forgive is to be imprisoned by the past, by old grievances that do not permit life to proceed with new business. Not to forgive is to yield oneself to another's control. The present is endlessly overwhelmed and devoured by the past. Forgiveness frees the forgiver.

What a marvelous picture of the therapeutic value of love in action. Active love, especially in the act of forgiveness, allows us to continue the walk of life. It enables us to live today to the fullest and move toward tomorrow. In giving up control—the right to hold others accountable for wrongs—love actually gives us back our lives, which we surrendered to objects of our disdain.

On the rock band U2's album *Rattle and Hum,* great blues guitarist B. B. King sings a moving gospel song. He lists the shortcomings of his life. He enumerates the damage done in relationships—each time adding a refrain about his new life in which he says, "When love comes to town I want to jump that train, / when love comes to town I wanna catch that flame. / Maybe I was wrong to ever let you down, / but I did what I did before love came to town."

The good news is that Love himself has come to town.

Finally, our walk of life is marked by the signpost of peace. Peace is a quality that appears in life and relationships as we begin to look at life from the perspective of others.

World situations may change by the time this book has gotten into your hands, but we know that from World War II until 1990, the United States and the Soviet Union had a shaky relationship. We were perfect enemies—each able to devastate the other, each seeking to make life a little more difficult for the other, and certainly each despising the other's point of view.

Then, without warning, through a series of world events, the wall of animosity that had existed for decades between the two superpowers crumbled. There was a shocked recognition that we were both afraid of many of the same things. As we somehow, mysteriously, locked on to a mutual understanding of each other's perspective, there was a platform for peace.

It is similar in our relationships. As we respond to the weight of God's love in our lives and seek to even the scale that I talked about at the beginning of this chapter, we find ourselves trying to see things from the perspective of others.

Christ is the source of the walk of life. Along the way, we encounter signs that we are in fact responding to God's initiation of love in our lives. Those signposts are humility, gentleness, long-suffering, love, and peace. And that brings us to the shape of the walk of life. It shapes up as unity.

Unity is a way of thinking. It doesn't mean that we always think the same way or always agree with others. It is the presence of an atmosphere that embraces a variety of possibilities and a number of styles. Unity is a state in which a group of those responding to God's love places the priority of "I" and "me" in the context of "you" and "we." Self is no longer paramount. Our "good" becomes solidly linked to the common good.

The wonderful secret of the walk of life as it takes shape is that we truly find ourselves when we lose ourselves in community. Human beings are in the business of meaning-making. We find meaning when we bring all of who we are to the table and risk living in intimacy with others. To protect, defend, preserve, and cherish the self is to taste death in this lifetime. An article titled "Boomer Blues" by Martin E. P. Seligar in the October 1988 issue of *Psychology Today,* gave the following conclusion to research on meaning in life:

> Surely one necessary condition for finding meaning in our lives is an attachment to something larger than the lonely self. To the extent that people now find it hard to take seriously their relationship with God, to care about their relationship with the country or community or to be a part of a large and abiding family, they will find it very difficult to find meaning in life. To put it another way, the self is a very poor site for finding meaning.

I opened this chapter with a French proverb and a quote from the Psalms. The proverb—"You not only have to want what you want, but you have to want what your wants lead to"—begs us to consider the walk of life as opposed to the emptiness of a life-style without spiritual texture and biblical underpinnings. To say no to the walk of life is to encounter the reality of living by shortsighted wants as depicted in the psalm ". . . So God gave them what they asked for, but sent a wasting disease upon them."

9 Measuring Up

But to each one of us grace has been given as Christ apportioned it. This is why it says: "When he ascended on high, he led captives in his train and gave gifts to men." (What does "he ascended" mean except that he also descended to the lower, earthly regions? He who descended is the very one who ascended higher than all the heavens, in order to fill the whole universe.) It was he who gave some to be apostles, some to be prophets, some to be evangelists, and some to be pastors and teachers, to prepare God's people for works of service, so that the body of Christ may be built up until we all reach unity in the faith and in the knowledge of the Son of God and become mature, attaining to the whole measure of the fullness of Christ. Then we will no longer be infants, tossed back and forth by the waves, and blown here and there by every wind of teaching and by the cunning and craftiness of men in their deceitful scheming. Instead, speaking the truth in love, we will in all things grow up into him who is the Head, that is, Christ. From him the whole body, joined and held together by every supporting ligament, grows and builds itself up in love, as each part does its work.

EPHESIANS 4:7-16

Someone once said, "You can only be young once, but you can be immature forever." This has sort of been a lifetime challenge for me. Like Peter Pan's little friends, I want to go on singing, "I'll never grow up . . . I'll never grow up."

Needless to say, a biblical text on maturity was the last thing I wanted to run into. I have spent the better part of my life trying to measure up and feeling like a failure. I have often resigned myself to a state of eternal adolescence. Many people feel in control of life. Not me. I once heard a metaphoric description of life that suits me perfectly. I am like a rodeo bull rider. Every day when the horn goes off, I come flying out of the chute and just try to hold on for eight seconds until the buzzer sounds. For me, life is a wild ride.

I am overwhelmed by my own shortcomings and crushed under the weight of the expectations of others. I have a wonderful story that tells just how far I have to go in the process of "measuring up" that Paul outlines in Ephesians 4:7–16. It happened on business in Atlanta. I had flown kitty-corner across America. It was late. I was beat. My business associate and I had a video crew with us and a load of heavy gear. We went to the rental-car desk at the Atlanta airport only to be told that the van we had reserved was not available. There were no cars. I was outraged. I demanded relief. The folks behind the desk shrugged. My anger grew.

Meanwhile, my calm and always adaptable associate, Jim, whom I dearly love for his gentle spirit and self-effacing style, is at another car-rental counter. While I am demanding my rights, he has cut a deal for a van that is larger, newer, and twenty-five dollars cheaper with no mileage limitations on it. I don't want that van. I want a van from the original car company.

Finally, Jim said, "I think the Lord really provided us with a great deal. What a gift." At last I caught on. I had been overwhelmed by my own sense of anger and need. I was literally behaving like an infant. I almost missed God's gift of grace.

My struggles to make life work, typified by my Atlanta experience, point out to me why God gives us community. You see, we all experience God's grace in different ways—and through our experience of grace, through our native temperaments and our portfolio of life experiences, God calls us to roles in community. Paul's list in Ephesians contains apostles, prophets, teachers, and pastors. It might well include other roles such as administrator and encourager.

The point is that God is in the business of distributing us in all our diverse gifts among each other. When projects need to be sold or client issues come up, I do a good job in my business. When change and adaptation are the issues, my partner, Jim, is the man for the moment.

The same is true of my marriage. Nancy is clearly more skilled than I am in many areas of our life together.

It is also true of many groups of Christians who are gathered to serve in churches and in organizations like Young Life or Fellowship of Christian Athletes. As Christians, we need to become a community where we can exercise our gifts and talents. We also need to become a community where we can allow others to bring their gifts to the places where we are deficient.

The other point that Paul makes right off the top in Ephesians 4 is that God has identified intimately with our human community in the person of Jesus Christ, and that Jesus, who is now the risen Lord, still possesses the sensitivity to us that he did in his time on earth. Out of that sensitivity he balances and counterbalances us with others. In other words, he distributes various roles among us to cause us to be mutually nurturing to each other.

And to what purpose? Well, it seems evident from Paul's understanding that the end result is the communal strength that is expressed in unity and the individual strength that is expressed in maturity. We "measure up" when we accept both our strengths and our weaknesses and then contribute those to the larger community where we are balanced out by others.

God gives us grace—and then gives us each other. Every person is unique. Everyone is gifted. Further, everyone is given a "measure" of giftedness. That means that no matter how gifted we may think we are or may appear—no matter how awesomely gifted someone else may look—all of us are limited. We need each other to reach maturity. Our personal strength can only take us so far toward fulfillment; then we need to be supplemented by others in the unity of community.

The Church of the Savior in Washington, D.C., has a wonderful line in its charter. It says, "On the ship of the church there are no passengers. All members are crew." So, just as we are checked by the fact that our gifts and talents are "measured," we are motivated by the fact that "to each is given." This is one of the paradoxes that we learn to live with if we want to be spiritually centered people. We must adopt the slogan: "I can't do it all, but I must do my part."

I want to reflect on yet another texture in this rich passage. Paul writes that all gifts, all roles, all opportunities for interaction in community are intended to build and strengthen the community. That says that as we grow and measure up, we will measure the effective use of our gifts, not by their demonstration, but by using those gifts as tools for service. The only posture acceptable for leadership in God's kingdom is service. The true measure of our gifts is how effective they are in building up other people.

John Calvin understood the need for leadership to be placed in the context of service and maximizing others. He said, "If we want to be considered members of Christ, let no one be anything for himself, but let us all be whatever we are for the benefit of each other."

It is important to remember who we are and what we are here for. The old adage that "we get so up to our ears in alligators that we forget that our object is to drain the swamp" is quite accurate. So often, we miss the core of life by getting caught up in our own needs. We get overwhelmed with the drive to be somebody, to belong, to control, to be cared for and affirmed. All those needs are valid, but they are not valid ends. They are results of a healthy process that recognizes that God has given us to each other for mutual nurture and empowerment. If I could just understand this, I would quit living life like the rodeo bull rider. I would look at the challenge of no rental car available at one counter as an opportunity to see God at work in my life.

Paul emphasizes that leaders are to build up the body of Christ. What a great test of leadership. Are things stronger because of his or her presence here? That doesn't fit well with our usual notions of judging leadership by how beautiful or popular someone is. The true test of leadership is best administered after the leader has left the scene.

I recently finished ten wonderful years in a church with a pastor who is, in my opinion, one of the best there is. I thought he was a gifted, visionary leader and enabler all along. He's gone now. He's pastoring another church. But even in his absence the church continues to grow in numbers, in outreach, in service, and in developing new leadership. That's the mark of world-class leaders! Things flourish after they are gone.

Science fiction writer H. G. Wells said, "Leaders should lead as far as they can and then vanish. Their ashes should not choke the fire they have lit." This pastor understood the message of Ephesians. Legitimate leadership empowers. Good leaders tend to diminish their control while at the same time their followers' power intensifies. This is a hallmark of good leadership. Great leaders build great leaders. It's a cycle.

Paul understood how passionate God is to restore this hurting and broken world. Ephesians 4:12 talks about all gifts working to "prepare God's people for works of service." The verb to prepare had an interesting usage in Greek. It means literally "to put right." It was used to describe a physician's act of setting a broken bone or a fisherman's act of repairing a broken net. Essentially, leadership gifts in the community, both those that we receive and those that we exercise, are specifically given to empower us in partnership with God.

Much has been said about spiritual gifts in the last several years. There is a powerful "signs and wonders" movement sweeping the country, emphasizing the "sign" gifts of the Holy Spirit such as tongues, healing, and prophecy. I do not decry the movement. I do not deny the gifts. But if my reading of Ephesians is correct, it is clear that the service gifts are the ones close to the core of God's plan.

That brings me to my next point. It is not an easy point for some to accept, but I believe it nonetheless. All Christians are commissioned to be leaders in their world. Each of us is to be a change agent and healer. There is no option. As I read Ephesians, I see a universal imperative in the text. All believers are to embark upon a spiritual and social journey that places them in various leadership roles, each according to his or her unique personality. Now, some of us lead and just don't know it. One business associate of mine can direct a broadcast with six cameras and a huge crew on hand. Every crew member is invigorated and affirmed by this guy. He is a gem! But he's quiet—and claims that he can't lead. Baloney!

On the other hand, I often encounter Christians who take no responsibility to lead by serving—whether in their families, job, church, or community. They say that's a job for someone else. Yet, so often these folks wind up in a counseling session with me or some other pastor telling about how their life isn't working and their faith is letting them down. I'm sorry, but I think that they are letting their faith down. Then there are those who loudly proclaim their leadership prowess but who are in actuality just noisemakers. They do not understand nurturing. They only understand pontificating and overpowering to attain their goals. Neither the self-aggrandizing nor the self-minimizing leader is a proper response to God's work in the deepest part of our lives.

I am convinced that assuming leadership roles is a risky act of spirituality. It is as essential to spirituality as prayer, worship, and taking communion. As we put our faith on the line and risk ourselves, we become stronger. To quote Paul, we become "sound"—or sturdy.

When Paul talks about maturity, he talks about reaching a point where we are not "tossed back and forth by the waves, and blown here and there by every wind of teaching and by . . . cunning." Paul's description of being tossed about conjures the image of a spinning top wildly out of control, or perhaps a ship adrift in a sea of nonmeaning. Outside of service in a unified community, we are without mooring.

Further, we are subject to all kinds of lies concerning what life is really about. The word *cunning* in our text is taken from the Greek word *kybea* and it refers to cheating at dice. Set adrift from solid community and disconnected from service, we are rendered susceptible to anything that sounds or looks good. We begin to live a lie. We lie to ourselves about who we are, we call God a liar by denying him the right to have the final word in our lives, and we begin living out the lie to others.

Paul's method of avoiding the wind and waves is to come close to God, accept the person he has made us to be, then begin sharing ourselves meaningfully and constructively with others. In this model we speak the truth, declaring who God is and who we are. We give God the last word, and we are authentic with others.

The ultimate image of the Church or body of Christ is of a bunch of independently actualized individuals choosing voluntarily and intentionally to become an interdependent organism. Each member contributes all that she or he has to create a healthy union and successfully functioning body.

Are you mature? Do you measure up? I don't. But I think that's okay. We're in process and what we have received from the apostle Paul in this section of Ephesians is a wonderful glimpse of the possibilities for us as we give ourselves to God and to each other. Maturity takes time. God is patient.

It's all right to grow slowly even though we live in a seven-minute society in which, I have heard it said, we can reach twenty-four thousand miles per hour, the velocity needed to escape Earth's atmosphere for space travel. In seven minutes we can pretty much microwave a flock of sheep, read how to be seven times the manager we were before, or take in all the headlines from around the world. Fine.

But God is not on a seven-minute agenda. He deals with chunks of time in decades, aeons, eternity. Thank goodness. I'm growing up. I'll write you when I get there.

10 Living in Light

So I tell you this, and insist on it in the Lord, that you must no longer live as the Gentiles do, in the futility of their thinking. They are darkened in their understanding and separated from the life of God because of the ignorance that is in them due to the hardening of their hearts. Having lost all sensitivity, they have given themselves over to sensuality so as to indulge in every kind of impurity, with a continual lust for more. You, however, did not come to know Christ that way. Surely you heard of him and were taught in him in accordance with the truth that is in Jesus. You were taught, with regard to your former way of life, to put off your old self, which is being corrupted by its deceitful desires; to be made new in the attitude of your minds; and to put on the new self, created to be like God in true righteousness and holiness. Therefore each of you must put off falsehood and speak truthfully to his neighbor, for we are all members of one body. "In your anger do not sin": Do not let the sun go down while you are still angry, and do not give the devil a foothold. He who has been stealing must steal no longer, but must work, doing something useful with his own hands, that he may have something to share with those in need. Do not let any unwholesome talk come out of your mouths, but only what is helpful for building others up according to their needs, that it may benefit those who listen. And do not grieve the Holy Spirit of God, with whom you were sealed for the day of redemption. Get rid of all bitterness, rage and anger, brawling and slander, along with every form of malice. Be kind and compassionate to one another, forgiving each other, just as in Christ God forgave you.

EPHESIANS 4:17-32

I remember a story from the news several years ago about a preadolescent boy who was flying a small plane with his father. The dad had a sudden heart attack and died. The desperate son took the radio in his hand and called for help. The people at a control tower gave him the confidence to attempt getting the plane under control. They bolstered him up and then began to give directions based upon his approximate location. They told the young man how the various controls worked and had him do some practice. They began to tell him which way to turn certain controls and how much as they guided him back toward the airfield from which the flight had originated. Among the final instructions was, "Now, son, if you've done all those things we told you to do, you should be able to look ahead and see a long black runway strip up ahead with some hills off to the left." The boy had manipulated the craft correctly—and as a result, his actions equaled "runway in sight."

Paul's formula is very similar to the one with which that young, distressed pilot worked. If a certain set of events takes place, you should wind up at a certain destination. Paul is saying that if God has done some deep things in our lives, then our responses should look like the virtues on the right side of Paul's formula.

We who spend a good bit of our time inside the church and have done so for many years have become accustomed to much "programmed religion" or formula Christianity. If you are like me, you tend to reject that mind-set. My tendency is to want to just let it go and let it flow.

So it's a little shocking when we run headlong into this passage of Scripture where the apostle Paul seems to be giving us a formula. Paul winds up for the pitch in apostolic fashion by insisting that followers of Christ do their part in living out the New Creation. They can no longer live like pagans if Christ has been at work in their lives. Eight verses later the apostle throws in the other half of the equation to complete his formula. He has a very specific quantity of behaviors that lie on the right side of a grammatical "equals" sign—a "therefore" at verse 25.

Before we get in too far, I want to confess my relative incompetence in mathematics. I am barely beyond the basics. But this one thing I know: if an equals sign separates two parts of an equation, the two sides are identical in quantity. The discipline called logic, which takes us beyond math, says that even though two quantities are identical, the two sides of the equation need not be identical in "form." That means that we have to be careful to read the equation from left to right, not right to left. This is a very important equation to memorize. It is essential to understanding much of what the remainder of Ephesians has to say to us.

Paul's formula Christianity begins with deep and significant activity by the power of the Holy Spirit on the left side of the grammatical equation and results in a set of measurable behaviors on the right side. To move the behaviors to the left side of the equation does not create a deep work of God. On the contrary, what we have created is legalism, stoicism, self-help—or even the New Age movement.

Such a thought system—one that is "religious"—is what Jesus came to abolish. Religion is a funny word. It comes from Latin. It means "to bind." While God has plans for you and me that spell freedom and fulfillment, the plan of religion is to bind. To seek

God's favor by religious behavior is oppressive to the soul. It ruins lives.

Jesus really disliked religiosity and moral one-upmanship. He told religious zealots, "You strain a gnat and swallow a camel." Jesus meant that when we become religious in our outlook, the details become so important that the overall point of life is missed. What a tragedy. Yet it is a frequent occurrence for many Christians who begin on the right path with a deep and centering relationship with Christ and sadly abandon that relationship for a much safer form of self-determined outward piety.

I need to stress a point before we delve any farther into Paul's formula. To say that if God has touched a person by his grace, then that person will show the following signs of growth as a response is not legalistic—it is a litmus test. But you cannot reverse the equation. Just because a person exhibits behaviors that appear godly does not assure that the person is intimately related to Christ. It is possible to look very religious on the outside and be very spiritually lost on the inside.

Tragically, when we Christians observe that our behavior has fallen short of what God has in mind for us, we tend to try to justify our bad behavior, or we attempt to muster all our energies to be good boys and girls, motivated by guilt and shame, in order that we might get some pie-in-the-sky heavenly dessert. But guilt and shame are horrible motivators. They are the twin towers of immobilizing power in many of our lives. Guilt and shame move us to do much of what we do, yet seldom do they move us in the right direction. I may go out and serve dinner to the homeless out of my sense of worthlessness, but when I get home I still feel like a loser. The issue is not what we do, but the center from which we do what we do.

I am convinced that the Holy Spirit is beckoning us from much deeper inside and offering much more significant and satisfying motivation to us. But we must get past the noise of guilt and shame to hear the Spirit. That means that we have to deal with guilt and shame when they come by recognizing that we are all sinners. Then we must deal with the sin, rather than being immobilized by guilt and shame.

A healthier reaction as we are confronted with our sin is exactly that which happened when men and women of old looked at the Ten Commandments: we are devastated by our inability to save ourselves and we run to Christ for mercy. It is at this point of admitting need and coming to Christ that we open ourselves to a new dose of the Holy Spirit and another round of battle between the New Creation and the old person.

This is a difficult sort of spirituality because it places us face to face with God. We find ourselves standing naked in front of the only One who can make us whole.

God in Christ communicates to us from within. Most of us are out of touch because we are too distracted to hear God speak. Just as it says in verse 19, we have "lost all sensitivity." This being the case, we are out of touch with the Lord, cut off from the internal control tower. Instead, we listen to loud and deceitful desires. We are drawn to the things that say they will fulfill us when their actual long-term result is to drain and deprive us of life.

I can still remember as a little boy how I would save up my pennies to buy a new "thing." Oftentimes this was some toy that I thought I absolutely had to have. Once I owned the toy, I realized several things. One, I was out of money. Two, the toy wasn't so great. Three, I felt stupid for wasting my money on the toy. Four, I felt emptier in the end than I had when I was still longing to own the toy.

I think this is a model of how many of us live our lives even as adults, moving from one longing to another through deep troughs of disappointment and self-contempt over the choices we have made. We become trapped in an endless cycle of expectations and letdowns.

An alternative to this draining behavior is to develop a life that includes reflection. I refer to the act of sitting quietly and listening to our own feelings, to the noise that is inside us. Then at the next stage, reflection is offering to God all of what we have discovered inside us, and sitting silently, in solitude in his presence, awaiting his love and direction. Living reflectively is the hardest of all life's labors. It's tough because we have to face our real selves and a very real God when most of us would prefer to drown out both things with superficial noise and activity. Reality is just a little too painful for most of us, but the path of reality, with all its pain, is the only road to wholeness.

This is frightening business. Dealing with our junk is like being lost in a dark jungle. Doing it alone, without the illumination of the Spirit, is an invitation to disaster. A classic devotional book called *The Cloud of Unknowing* says that "a candle is seen by the burning thereof." The wonder of faith in God is that as we put our lives on the line and really begin to examine ourselves, we, the candle, are viewed by the light of our burning. The Holy Spirit burning within the center of our lives illuminates our path to wholeness and spiritual maturity. Self-directed searches are literally a shot in the dark.

Most of us, if we are honest, will admit that we are given to an attitude of self-reliance. Hope becomes a function of how our organism is functioning at any given moment. Stressful days, headaches, sickness, relational troubles, or career frustrations tend to color our sense of hope daily or hourly. Small setbacks and irritations cast us into the pits. The horizon of self-defined hope is very close. I enjoy river rafting very much. But I am always amazed by how little world you can see and how few daylight hours there are when you are floating along in a deep canyon. To be made new in the mind is to become one who begins to think with eternal perspective rather than with a boxed-canyon myopia. A life of reflection can be revolutionary for us if it is mixed with an eternal perspective.

We know that in large measure we choose how to behave. All of us have had the experience of saying, "I am going to be angry. I am going to be an absolute creep, and nothing anyone does will change it." We've all done that—choosing to be foul even when there are some encouraging things around us that might draw us to a better disposition. Well, what we see here is a self-deceptive, self-determined choice to live below one's resources. Paul says, "Put on the new self"—give it a try and see what happens rather than choosing to grovel. We can choose a spiritual path, a path that depends upon God for the resources of strength, perspective, and hope. This is not a path that is determined by exertion of the will, but rather by a surrender to grace.

Paul makes reference to three of our internal issues: desire, attitude, and motivation. This is the place where the Holy Spirit comes to work inside each person who believes. Then, on the other side of his equals sign at verse 25 is an imposing list of behaviors. Paul is saying: "If you have submitted to God's deep working within you, here is what you should be seeing." The virtues Paul lists are not necessarily in prioritized order, but it is amazing to me how much they relate to psychological standards for a well-adjusted person:

A fearless commitment to honesty. This is one of the very first commitments people in Alcoholics Anonymous must make. They must stop lying to themselves and others. They must begin calling a spade a spade. So it is with what I would call "Sinners Anonymous." All of us who aspire to follow Christ and live the adventure of life to the fullest must commit to becoming transparent people. We must, in computer graphics terms, become WYSIWYG people. WYSIWYG means "what you see is what you get."

A commitment to deal directly with anger. We cannot let anger become a random toxic spill. Some of us experience anger more strongly and more frequently than others, but all of us know how anger feels. It burns. It screams for justice, for revenge. It senses a wound inflicted so acutely that it seeks to wound in return.

Anger is toxic. Just as we have kidneys in our bodies to remove toxins, we have systems to deal with anger emotionally and spiritually. Emotionally, we deal with anger by not denying it. We accept that we are angry. We don't misdeliver our anger to a wrong address. We express our anger to the one who has made us angry. We express anger in the first person, "I am angry because I feel . . .," rather than placing the blame on the one with whom we are angry.

It's our anger. We own it. Spiritually, we deal with anger by giving it up. We surrender it to God for our own good and the good of the planet. We let go. We forgive. We move ahead knowing that we, too, have been the source of anger on many occasions. Most of all, as Paul says, we deal with anger by keeping short accounts. We get angry without sinning by taking care of business right away.

A commitment to meaningful work. We need to serve to better society as a whole, not just to enhance the individual. Paul says, "He who has been stealing must steal no longer, but must work." Our work and our presence in the community are conceived as part of a much greater scheme than our personal goals and wishes. We see our work as a contribution to the common good, our energies as an offering for the betterment of all. Our vocation in the world is an expression of our spirituality. What we do is as much offered to God as our prayers or worship.

Therefore, we do what we do with passion and determination. We do our life's work with a sense of calling. We select our life's work with a sense of purpose in mind. So, it would be impossible to be a thief and make ill-gotten gains an offering to God. Likewise, it would be impossible to work in a job that oppresses others. Our spending of life's energy day in and day out is a holy call from God. When we understand and live that, we move closer to being fully integrated persons.

A commitment to uphold the dignity of others. We perceive other people as valuable, significant persons, worthy of respect and understanding. We watch what we say and do. We do so for the benefit of others. Our desire is to build, strengthen, and affirm others. Our words should be used to that end and no other. The same goes for our activities. Paul even uses the example of brawling to show how we should not act. You don't break bottles over people's heads.

A commitment to self-respect. When we care about ourselves, we open ourselves to caring for others. We possess a sense of self-worth that naturally leads us to affirm the worth of others rather than to adopt a competitive, "put-down" attitude. As we respect others we look for ways to be kind. We seek to capture the essence of who people are and where they are going. We allow for their uniqueness rather than trying to shoehorn everyone into our mold.

A commitment to compassion. Compassion frees others from our expectations and allows them to be who and what they are. When we see the shortcomings, failures, and inadequacies of others, are we led to be judgmental, condemning, or even cruelly amused? I think all too often this is the case. God's vision for us is that we would respond to his tenderness and understanding in our lives with a good dose of tenderness and understanding toward others.

Compassion moves us to respond to the situation of others. As we see sin and failure, God does not need us to play judge and jury. He has the right to do that and chooses to pass on the court proceedings. He reacts in sorrow. Sin and failure hurt God every time he sees them. He hurts for what such things do in the lives of people who are precious to him. Compassion is borrowing God's looking glass and viewing people the way he views them.

If you take this list and make an archetypal person of it, you see a mature, sensitive, spiritually aware individual who is strong from the inside out—very able to cope with his or her environment. That is what it means to be a child of God—a New Creation.

What is taking place deep inside us is in harmony with God's plan to restore an entire discordant and fallen universe into a symphony of praise to him. Furthermore, the model we see in this passage robs the enemy of our souls of any foothold. Paul is acutely aware that there is evil in the world. It is real. It is personal. His name is Satan and he is ever searching to corrupt God's creation.

Responding to God's deep work in our lives by the Holy Spirit denies evil any place to attach itself or operate efficiently through us. Anger, fear, anxiety, guilt, and shame are five rungs on a ladder leading to our personal "control center." Grace gives entry and authority over that control center to Jesus Christ and removes the ladder upon which evil ascends.

If you look at the dark side of this list of behaviors in Ephesians 4:17–32, the negative behaviors so many of us struggle with, you see sin in action, destroying the world. You see a focus on others—an overbearing set of expectations, selfishness, and hypersensitivity. You read the list and get a picture of an organism that provides many points of contact for the evil that stalks our planet. It is a list of behaviors that invites corruption and decay. This is a list with which most of us are all too well acquainted. It's sad that we own this list of attributes because we are too afraid to open ourselves to the possibility of grace through the discipline of reflection.

Let me make a suggestion. Go to a quiet place where you can tune others out, and read the passage from Ephesians at the beginning of this chapter. Marvel at the depths inside of you at which God is poised to go to work. Then look at the right side of the equation.

How do you stack up? Most of us don't score too well. Once you have done your inventory, realize that there are three choices. *One* is to rationalize your shortcomings, blaming God and the rest of the world for not doing things your way. *Another* is to bludgeon and beat yourself for your shortcomings and try your best to muster up willpower and moral courage to get the job done and make the virtues yours.

The *last* and certainly the only workable option is to come home to Christ. Open the deepest parts of yourself to him. Develop sensitivity to him speaking inside you. Give Christ time. Let him help you stop fooling yourself. Let Christ give you new eyes to see the world and take the first step in a New Walk of Life. Christ is the ingredient you need to make Paul's formula for the Christian life work.

11 The Imprint

Be imitators of God, therefore, as dearly loved
children and live a life of love, just as Christ
loved us and gave himself up for us as a fragrant
offering and sacrifice to God. But among you
there must not be even a hint of sexual immorality, or of any kind of impurity, or of greed,
because these are improper for God's holy people. Nor should there be obscenity, foolish talk
or coarse joking, which are out of place, but
rather thanksgiving. For of this you can be sure:
No immoral, impure or greedy person—such a
man is an idolater—has any inheritance in the
kingdom of Christ and of God. Let no one de-
ceive you with empty words, for because of such
things God's wrath comes on those who are disobedient. Therefore do not be partners with
them.

EPHESIANS 5:1-7

For a good part of my early adult life I worked as a disc jockey
on rock-and-roll radio stations. I love music and I loved
being involved right in the heart of our culture. I met many
great people. I learned a lot. I saw a lot. Some good and some bad.
I tried my best to live authentically and, although I made some terrible mistakes, I also had some moments of getting to live publicly
as a Christian.

During my radio days, I had opportunities to interact with different philosophies of life. In the seventies and eighties there was a good deal of talk about guilt. People were saying in magazines and in the songs I played on the radio that guilt was bad. I agreed to a certain extent. Many of us are overly guilty or carry false guilt. For those of us in that category, guilt can be negative. But for others of us, guilt can be a good thing.

I mention my radio career because I had one of the few poignant insights of my life while on the air. I was interacting with the news anchor whom we called Flash. Flash was doing a "down with guilt" story that even he couldn't believe. I popped the microphone open and said, "You know, Flash, I think guilt is the smoke alarm of our lives." Flash responded, "Huh, uh, um." "Guilt," I continued, "is there to tell us that we violated a moral standard we believe to be true." Flash said, "Yeah, I see what you mean." We went on to have a humorous conversation about smoke alarms and even talked about how to install them.

Here's the point. Guilt can and does function as the smoke detector in our lives. God gives us his Spirit in our inner person. When we violate the way he wants us to live in order to have a fulfilling life experience and be beneficial to others in this world, the alarm goes off. God smells smoke. Where there is smoke, there is fire, the adage goes. And where there is fire, there is destruction.

Imagine that the smoke alarm goes off where you live. It is signaling a fire that has been caused by faulty wiring in your abode. What are your options? You can respond to the alarm and deal with the fire. Or you can run down the hall, pull the cover off the alarm, and remove the battery so the obnoxious thing stops honking. What are you going to do? Very few of us would remove the battery and let the building burn down around us. Yet, when it comes to God correcting us morally because our lives are on fire, we resent it. We choose to disable the smoke alarm and shut God out. We cover our ears to block out the noise. We hide. We say, "No, that's not a smoke alarm, that's just my stereo playing."

Now remember, I am not an advocate of false guilt. In our house the darned smoke alarm goes off frequently when we are baking or even when we are making popcorn. In that case, we just remove the battery for a moment. We have analyzed the situation. There is no fire. We cut off the alarm, but then a few minutes later we put the battery back and return the smoke alarm to its sentry duty. All of us can learn to distinguish a real from a false alarm and then act appropriately. But just because we occasionally get false alarms doesn't mean that we discard the system!

As we read Paul's opening words to the fifth chapter of Ephesians, it is critical that we understand the role that God plays in our lives when it comes to informing our morality. Paul understands clearly: if God is at work inside us, some things are going to show up on the outside as a result.

For some of us who grew up in the Woodstock sixties and disco seventies with lots of alternative life-style exploration, especially of our sexuality, we have discovered a problem as we approach our faith. We find it difficult to define the nature of relational intimacy. Some of us have trouble discovering a conscience inside of us.

Most of us were raised with a strong sense of morality that parallels the biblical model that we are now reading about in Ephesians. The problem is, many of us were taught the morals in an inflexible and "hung-up" way. When we rejected those morals and began to experiment with new values, there was guilt and shame. We learned not to hear the guilt and shame by sheer force of repeating the new behaviors. But, in the process, we messed up the wiring. Now, as we approach faith in Christ, we are struggling with the moral deadness or ambivalence we are experiencing.

The good news is that God is very comfortable being in the restoration business. Over time, God can rebuild our disconnected consciences. A God-driven conscience is a "Cadillac" smoke alarm. I came out of the sixties a mess. I worked hard to become "free" and lawless. I am still a bit of a rebel. When I became a Christian I was afraid of how all the morality issues would affect me. I was worried about buying into an oppressive moral system.

What I found was quite the opposite. I discovered a living relationship with Christ—the same Christ who lived on earth as Jesus of Nazareth and faced the same temptations that human beings face. He didn't give in. But he sure knows how easy it is to buy into the world's system of morality.

My sense of how Christ deals with me is that he tenderly understands me in my mistakes. That means that God is patient and gentle in restoring us. I have discovered over the last twenty years that it is a joyful thing to have a God-built conscience. It's not like the Jiminy Cricket morality that we got as kids—you know, when Jiminy sits on your shoulder and gently harangues you into good behavior. Rather, it is deeply personal. It is also morality with a purpose.

When I blow it, I don't hear God screaming at me. I hear a gentle voice saying that I have inflicted damage on myself or another. And I have come to know the gift of repentance.

Repentance comes from a Greek word that means "to turn around" or "change one's mind." It is wonderful to know what to do when I fail morally. I used to have to try to bury the feelings, or redefine my values, rationalize, or project my failures onto someone else. Now I have a process of dealing with "life garbage" that is much more productive and fulfilling. I confess to God that I realize I have blown it. I take responsibility for myself. I ask forgiveness.

Then I sit silently for a few minutes and wait for a sense of cleansing. Next I await a strategy for a new direction (repent = turn around/change mind). Often I seek what I might need to do to restore a situation or relationship that I have damaged by my sin. Then I go away from that encounter with God nourished and energized to try again—with complete freedom to fail again. I say to myself, "If I keep coming back to life and trying and trying, again and again, someday I am bound to get it right."

The act of responding to God's voice inside us is what Paul refers to in the opening words of Ephesians 5 as being "imitators of

God." Remember that odd machine called a mimeograph that made smelly copies you and your classmates sniffed in grade school? It was a copier that took an original imprint, added ink to it, and made massive copies of Dick and Jane lessons.

Well, the word *mimeograph* comes from the Greek word *mimeo,* which means to copy or "mimic." That is the same root word the apostle Paul uses in Ephesians 5:1. It is rich with imagery. Imagine getting so close to God in Christ that his essence, his character rubs off on you and leaves an indelible print. I like the concept. Again, we observe that Christian virtue is rooted in a response to intimacy with Christ, not in moral effort alone. In intimate relationship, God leaves the *imprint* of himself indelibly upon us.

Football coaches talk about being on the "same page" with players and other coaches. What they are referring to is being on the same page of the game plan. The game plan is a large book specifically designed to show every conceivable strategy in one particular game. The players and assistant coaches must all understand the same variables to get on the "right page" and call a successful play.

God asks us frequently if we are on the same page with him. Do we understand all the variables, all the facts surrounding our moral decisions and behaviors? We need to be close to him in prayer and reflection in order to be on the same page—in order for his style, his heart, his strategy to be imprinted on us.

If we are not intimately connected with God, we begin to shift on our foundation and become unstable. We remove ourselves from contact with the mimeograph. When that happens we are cut off from inheriting God's character and resources to assist us through our life journey. What I am concluding here is that immorality is a direct result of not being in relationship with God. It is a signal that we have chosen not to be connected. When that choice has been made we no longer have contact (as in mimeograph copies having contact with the master plate) and do not inherit or receive what is intended for us.

There has been much discussion through the years about the nature of evil. I believe the best definition of evil is that it is the natural result of the absence of good. In Christianity, we view good as the presence of God. Therefore, evil is the place or condition in which God's presence is not felt.

As we consider evil and good, we must also think about the issue of obedience that Paul addresses in Ephesians 5:1–7. Obedience is a tough word. We sometimes think of mindless compliance. We think of dog-training schools and concentration camps. But, given the perspective we have discussed in this chapter, the first act of obedience is simply to come into God's presence, to acknowledge him as the boss. Obedience is not at first an act of right behavior but a state of right relationship.

Paul hints at the relational nature of obedience at the end of our section of scripture for this chapter. In referring to the models of immorality in the world that would reinforce our poorest choices in life, he says, "Do not be partners with them." Paul is begging you and me to choose partnership with God rather than partnership with the various unproven and morally bankrupt voices of this world that dazzle us with "empty talk." The Greek word for empty in this passage means "vain" or "without purpose." The sense is that we are all stimulated by certain shortsighted ideas about how to make it through today and tonight.

For some of us, it is the appeal not to go home alone from the dance club. For others, it is the temptation to undermine someone at work because it will help our cause. For yet others, the vain talk will be from an advertisement in a magazine that beckons us to a local shopping mall to buy one more outfit or one more scent that will somehow fulfill our empty lives. Paul understands the vanity of shortsighted indulgences, as did the hymn writer who so aptly said, "All the vain things that charm me most, I sacrifice them. . . ." In an earlier chapter, I discussed not only wanting what we want but wanting what our wants lead to, and Paul has brought us back to that concept.

In Ephesians 5, the apostle's recommendation is that to avoid being trapped by the empty promises of quick-fix value systems, we focus on partnership with God and godly friends. I have confessed that I am a rebel. For years I have prided myself on walking at the edge. But let me tell you a secret. The thing that has freed me to work in the secular world of broadcasting is the fact that I have always done so with a strong understanding of who I am as God's child—and I have always had a marvelously supportive group of friends who love me and continuously model what it means to live honestly, openly, and in devotion to Christ. I have walked near the edge, but unseen to most was a group of mentors who coached me. My friends protected me the way spotters in a gymnastics meet protect someone from falling off the trampoline.

Unfortunately, I have seen many baby-boomer Christians stray too close to the edge without a spotter. Some have gone over. I have tragic memories of dear Christian friends whose partnership with the systems of this world resulted in public humiliation, moral ruin, suicide, and imprisonment. This is not just a list of negative circumstances; it is a list of people whom I have known and loved. The point here is that *staying* in relationship to Christ and godly significant others is the antidote for *straying* as we attempt to live purposefully, relevantly, and effectively in the world.

What I am reminding us of is the need to practice the first level of obedience. That is, to come to Christ continually, both with the challenges we face and with the failures we experience. We can come to him boldly. He can erase all damage we have done to ourselves, even though certain circumstances that resulted from our bad choices cannot be reversed. Some choices we make cause us to live with the consequences. For instance, we may choose to drive while intoxicated, which may result in a wreck that could harm us or others. That is something we have to live with. But God can even make something useful out of our permanent messes.

Please remember that even our moral failures can be used for our personal growth and for the benefit of others. I have seen many persons grow through divorce, bankruptcy, legal problems, and even criminal records. It is hard to imagine that we have a God who is masterful in pulling off major reconstruction jobs like those, but it is no pipe dream. I can guarantee by God's work in my own life and through my own failures that this is true. With courage, then, we can come near to God whether with the good or the bad stuff—and with confidence we can know that he accepts us and will work to good ends in our lives. Time spent with God leaves a good impression. In fact, it leaves a lasting impression on our inner person that is legible to the world as it permeates through to the outer person.

12   Travel Tips

For you were once darkness, but now you are light in the Lord. Live as children of light (for the fruit of the light consists in all goodness, righteousness and truth) and find out what pleases the Lord. Have nothing to do with the fruitless deeds of darkness, but rather expose them. For it is shameful even to mention what the disobedient do in secret. But everything exposed by the light becomes visible, for it is light that makes everything visible. This is why it is said: "Wake up, O sleeper, rise from the dead, and Christ will shine on you." Be very careful, then, how you live—not as unwise but as wise, making the most of every opportunity, because the days are evil. Therefore do not be foolish, but understand what the Lord's will is. Do not get drunk on wine, which leads to debauchery. Instead, be filled with the Spirit. Speak to one another with psalms, hymns and spiritual songs. Sing and make music in your heart to the Lord, always giving thanks to God the Father for everything, in the name of our Lord Jesus Christ.

EPHESIANS 5:8-20

Years ago, three of my friends decided to hop a slow-moving freight train on the south end of a town in the Pacific Northwest. It was supposed to be a lark on a spring evening. The train was barely moving.

As the three friends rode down the rails, the locomotive poured on the coals and really picked up speed. Before my friends knew it they were doing about forty miles per hour. They had left the city. Darkness was setting in out in the boondocks. Soon my three friends were cold, lost, and scared.

After half an hour or so, they decided that they had to do something. So in perfect Butch Cassidy fashion, they lined up in the door of the boxcar in which they were riding—and they bailed out. It was a rough tumble down into some bushes (several of which were blackberry vines), but my friends were okay. The problem was, they were terribly lost. It was pitch dark.

Eventually, one of the guys looked off in the distance and saw a faint glow. It looked like there was a small town out there. The three humiliated joyriders began walking through the woods. With each increment they traveled the light became brighter and more distinct. There was a town out there! Soon the light became intense enough to illuminate their path. They wound up at a roadside restaurant and called for help.

My friends got home safely because they saw a distant light and walked in its glow. It became an overwhelming beacon that led them to where they needed to go. This, to me, is a fine example of what it means to walk in the light.

In the previous chapter, we discussed what Paul meant by inviting us to be imitators of God. God invites us to receive the imprint of his character. In this chapter, we will look a little more closely at what it means to be disciples, or imitators, as we get some travel tips on how to move through the world in which we live. As I read Ephesians 5:8–20, two themes become evident: living in the "light" and living in "wisdom." These are two very important concepts.

In the story of Adam and Eve, I am always taken by one tragic episode in that first family's history. It typifies our human tendency to avoid the light of God's presence in our lives. The incident takes place after Adam and Eve have eaten fruit from the forbidden tree. They hear God coming into their garden home called Eden, and, ashamed of what they have done, self-conscious, wanting to hide their naked bodies from the One who created them, they conceal themselves in the bushes. When they are discovered by God, Adam confesses that he didn't want to be seen naked. His shame is multiplied as he recognizes his inability to hide from God, and an entire relationship becomes fouled by deception and rationalization, to the point that God actually sends Adam and Eve out of the garden and humankind's relationship with God is changed forever.

We read that primitive story and feel ourselves shudder. It is our story. We are not creatures who are naturally comfortable with the light. Light in this particular context has to do with honesty and accountability. Neither of those appeals to me. How about you? Honesty and accountability are tough principles to live by. We no longer have the final say on our behavior.

I have never been one who loves being called to account. Recently a co-worker confronted me on the fact that I had been talking too loudly on the phone and that, furthermore, he thought some of my conversation had been in objectionable taste.

I sat there as I was held accountable and I burned. I was mad at myself. I knew that my language had been coarse. I was having a bad day. To add to my shame at being out of line, I was determined to minimize my error by claiming that I was having a tough day and had a right to be crass. Furthermore, I resented any friend, foe, or bozo holding me accountable, even if what they said was true.

The process of living in the light does not mean accepting criticism or accountability without feeling any sting. I nearly always feel devastated. But I am also thankful for good friends and a forgiving God on the backside of a "flashlight" experience. These minicrises of accountability greatly enable growth in my life. The thing that's good about the process is that it functions as a spiritual chiropractic adjustment.

We get out of alignment through things like bad days. The more stress we encounter, the more we are likely to dredge up the dark side of our personalities. The same is true when we are depressed or angry. When we encounter the backside of our personalities, accountability that brings us into the light is a good thing. It is restorative. We are brought into check before our natural inclinations cause us to damage ourselves or someone else. I hate accountability . . . but I like the idea of walking in the light and have grown to view accountability as a gift.

Paul mentions in Ephesians 5 that light actually has power over the darkness. It has expulsive power. Where light goes, darkness disappears for the time that light is present. As God's Spirit and key friends bring light to my life, I am released from my dark side. Light is overpowering.

Paul mentions several monitoring points for walking in the light. They are goodness, righteousness, and truth. Earlier in Ephesians 5, we noted that someone in intimate relationship with Christ avoids off-color talk. When I was made accountable for my loud phone conversation, I was reminded of the standard of goodness. Goodness refers to moral excellence. Part of living in the light is being willing to cross-reference our behavior with biblically acceptable standards and further be willing to admit that we have fallen short.

Righteousness in the text for this chapter refers to the domain of right relationships. It means giving other people their due—treating them with the respect and dignity bestowed by their Creator. It means nurturing and affirming others. When we live in the light, we admit that we are accountable for maximizing others in the way we relate to them. Of course, righteousness has a direct relationship to goodness: we could not maliciously gossip against or slander someone (an unrighteous act) unless we were also failing to live out the concept of goodness.

Truth is the last element of the triumvirate that makes up living in the light. Truth means living genuinely, vulnerably. Truth is the act of being who and what we are at any moment. Truth means living without pretense. Truth is the act of admitting a failure to be good or righteous. Truth is revealing our motives. Truth is an act of self-acceptance and honest self-disclosure to others.

I often get in trouble with others because I attempt to live as though I have nothing to hide. Recently, at a Christian prayer gathering I admitted that the best motive I have ever had is a mixed motive and offered the idea that I think God accepts that. People were shocked. They really believed that they were capable of pure motives in living life. As we talked further, the group began to understand that declaring perfect purity puts one on shaky ground.

If you want to blow minds around you and also set people free, try telling the truth about yourself. It is a marvelous experience. The more secrets you feel you have to hold, the more those secrets hold you. In fact, we become what we hide. When I examine the shortcomings in my life and the flaws in my personality, I am shocked into wanting to get things out in the open and not become a living reflection of my dark side.

I remember the day a friend told a group of us that she had a speech impediment. Well, her speech impediment was so obvious, and we accept her in spite of it, that when she spoke up we all began to laugh. Her very confession was made with obvious evidence of her verbal flaw. It was not mocking laughter. It was the laughter of all of us recognizing how much we try to hide our various flaws, how much we are owned by those flaws.

The fact is that the chinks in our armor are eminently visible to those around us. When we try to hide them, we only fool ourselves—and perhaps make fools of ourselves.

As Paul continues with his travel tips for the Christian adventure, he moves to living in wisdom. Equipped with light to help us see our way through life, we are helped to choose the best path by living in wisdom.

Verse 16 of Ephesians 5 urges us to make the most of our time. The reason for this, according to Paul, is that we live in troubled times, evil days. Lots of distractions and unproductive opportunities tug at us. In the Greek, the word that we translate into "make the most" actually means "redeem." Paul is telling us to use our time like a coupon—to cash it in for a good return. What a great encouragement. I get a mental picture of waking up every day with a coupon in my hand worth a full, enjoyable, meaningful, and productive day. Whatever that day may involve—work or play, exercise, rest, reflection, or interpersonal relationships—it is worth something if I am willing to "redeem the time." I can make it count!

To use our time well and live meaningfully we must understand something about God's will. Wisdom is knowing the difference between good and best, and what better way to determine that than by working our way through life gaining knowledge about God's will. I think this is an area in which late-twentieth-century Christians are weak. We are scripturally illiterate and not theologically informed. This is a dangerous way to live. It is not wise.

The theologian Karl Barth said that every Christian who wants to live a full and meaningful life of faith should live with the Bible under one arm and the day's newspaper under the other. I think he meant that the two need to speak to each other. We need to submit the facts and events of our life experiences to the truths of Scripture and let the two interact. Sometimes it gets wild. What we experience and what the Bible says can wind up wrestling with each other—a process wherein we are greatly enriched.

I have especially found this in the area of human conflict. My tendency is to justify my side of things and talk about interpersonal problems with all but the people involved. Sound familiar? Scripture says no to my tendency. It shows me a better way.

The idea of Bible study or theological study may sound beyond your reach, but believe me, it isn't. Purchase one good Bible-study aid to help you learn one book of the Bible, such as the Gospel of Mark, and you will emerge with not just a solid understanding of Mark, but also a pretty good knowledge of the Gospels in general. I still remember how my concept of who Jesus is was forever changed through my study of Mark. I was overwhelmed with Jesus' personal strength combined with his enormous compassion for the down-and-outers of the world.

As you spend time studying, you will gain a wealth of knowledge about Bible-study methods and biblical interpretation. It's fun. And it isn't beyond anyone. Theology is equally easy to learn. You can buy very simple books about the character of God or the person of Christ that will build your mind and deepen your spirituality.

Another way to grow in knowing God's will is simply to spend time with God in prayer. Ask his will on the issues in your life and patiently wait in silence for a sense of what is right. Then, just for confirmation, check out what you are feeling with some mature Christian friends. It is wonderful to break out of our time-locked experience and tap into God's eternal perspective on life. With God's Word and a group of Christian friends we can begin to live in confidence.

The third element of living in wisdom is being filled with God's Spirit. The mathematician and philosopher Blaise Pascal observed that there is a God-shaped vacuum in each of our hearts, and it was Augustine who, earlier in history, said that all our hearts are restless until they find their rest in God. What these great thinkers were saying is that we all have a need to experience God. We desire to sense God's presence. As we grow spiritually by spending time with God in prayer and reflection, we become sensitive to the Holy Spirit's presence in our lives. That presence is inspiring and comforting. It fulfills our deepest longings. It is a source of peace, and also a source of discomfort when we have crossed acceptable boundaries.

Being full of the Spirit is being so immersed in our relationship with Christ that we sense God with us outside of our quiet prayer times. We experience God in all our acts: in our hands as we do physical work, in our minds as we pursue professional occupations, in our relationships as we deal with people, in our play as we shoot a basketball or ski down a snowy hillside in crisp winter air. I loved the movie *Chariots of Fire*. When the main character, Eric Liddell, is urged to give up a promising running career to be a pastor, he responds, "When I run, I feel His pleasure."

I can relate. I have felt God's pleasure when I was on the radio as a disc jockey or doing play-by-play announcing for a sports event. I have felt God's pleasure in times of conversation with my daughter, Rachel. It's great to experience being full of the Holy Spirit. It is not always a peak experience, one where we intensely feel God's presence, but it is a very real gift offered to those who live in relationship with Christ. God's presence provides a baseline for daily existence to play upon.

Paul's discussion of living in light and living in wisdom ends on a somber note. He adjures each of us to "be careful, then, how you live." Paul's travel tips encourage us to live intentionally—to live with care. That doesn't mean paranoia or overexamination, but it does mean to live as if life is worth something.

So much of our society is afraid of living and afraid of dying, stuck in the mud of meaninglessness and despair. God says we don't have to live that way. We can enjoy a great trip. Here are some summary tips:

1. Living intentionally brings meaning to our lives. Socrates said that the unexamined life is not worth living. Life without a goal or an end is useless. When we live intentionally we seek God's guidance in setting very clear goals for our lives, and then we seek his assistance and direction in attaining those goals. Living intentionally goes beyond setting career and financial goals. It includes setting family, friendship, service, spiritual, and psychological goals as well.

2. Self-examination is critically important. We needn't become terminal navel-gazers, but we should take regular time to examine our lives spiritually, psychologically, morally, and socially. Where do I need to grow? How have I done? Part of this assessment is

accepting the progress we have made. Part of it is spotting areas that need to be addressed. Part of it is resting comfortably in the strengths we possess and the gifts God has given us.

3. Balance is essential. As we learn to set goals and examine our progress, we also learn to live loosely and flexibly. We grow in our acceptance of little surprises along the way in life.

4. We learn to live in community. We set goals, examine our lives, and balance our lives. We grow in a conscious devotion. We identify a few key friends who will be the important voices we listen to and whose advice we will take seriously.

5. We become stewards of all of life. The one who travels life well is the one who seeks to leave the planet a better place than it was before she or he entered it. Service to the world, positive social impact, is critical for living a life journey that is meaningful. Joy is found in making a difference.

6. We live from the inside out. We are increasingly aware of Christ as the center. We place the whole business of life in the context of a vital and continuous relationship with Jesus Christ. Goals, self-examination, balance, community, and service all have Christ and the building of his kingdom as their source, sustenance, and ultimate goal. Never allow any center for living other than the living Christ.

PART
FOUR

Introduction

As I read Ephesians 5:21–6:9 I observe the apostle Paul demanding that persons in Christ abandon roles and assume a posture of mutual submission. Ephesians 5:21 is the hinge verse for this entire section: "Submit to one another out of reverence for Christ."

This commandment is one of the hardest in all of Scripture. It is hard to measure, harder to enforce, hard to adapt to in a societal system that has been hierarchical. Paul's commandment creates tension—and sometimes even confusion—in us if we take it seriously, yet it is the only way for all persons to move through life and relationships with dignity. Relationships are not healthy when the dynamic of love is described as that which makes more of one party while the other party is diminished, or even demeaned. Love is meant to be mutually empowering. Mutual empowerment is the final goal of God's re-creation in human relationships. This mutual empowerment even carries over to the way that social institutions operate. It redefines the nature of power and authority. It cuts the age-old and sinful bonds of one human being having dominating power over another.

We must appreciate the God-given differences between genders. We must acknowledge the difference between those who are children and those who nurture them. We must accept the difference between those vocationally called to manage or lead and those vocationally called to skilled or technical positions that make them subordinates. Yet I am convinced of the need for mutual respect and deemphasis in the role distinction between such parties.

One critical ingredient in this next section is an understanding of the cultural context in which the letter to the Ephesians was written. I will refer a great deal to first-century Greco-Roman culture in the following three chapters. I must also add that cultural context forces us always to look at the original intent of the author of an ancient text and then translate it to our own culture. I have been practicing this throughout the course of the book. For instance, earlier I did this to describe the "sense" of the Greek word *hamartia* ("miss the mark"), which we translate in English as "sin."

Cultural context and cross-cultural translation become even more important as the apostle Paul, who began Ephesians by describing the activity of God by the Holy Spirit deep in our inner lives, begins to apply the outworking of God's grace to a specific culture. Is the Bible still God's authoritative word? Yes. Do we have to work a little to understand the meaning? By all means!

Now, you are probably familiar with the process of translating a text. First, one investigates the cultural context of the world in which the text was originally received. Second, one determines the author's original intent—his or her message to the particular culture to which he or she was writing. Third, one determines the universal message that transfers from the original culture to the culture in which one is living.

A friend of mine worked with a mission organization whose sole purpose was to translate the Bible and Christian literature into the languages of peoples who had never heard the Christian message. The organization sent a group of translators to a small and remote tribe in South America. When the translators reached the passage in the Gospel of John where Jesus speaks to a crowd saying, "I am the bread of life," they realized that there was no such thing as bread in that culture. The tribe used a specific kind of banana a

bit like we use bread. You've got it! "I am the banana of life" was the
culture-specific translation. That sounds silly or even blasphemous
to us—but it was the correct application of the timeless message
of God to the human race everywhere as applied in that one South
American tribe.

Armed with this understanding of culture, we can move on to
a challenging section of Ephesians and look for God's timeless
message to people who are approaching the year 2000.

13 Man and Wife or Man and Woman?

Submit to one another out of reverence for Christ. Wives, submit to your husbands as to the Lord. For the husband is the head of the wife as Christ is the head of the church, his body, of which he is the Savior. Now as the church submits to Christ, so also wives should submit to their husbands in everything. Husbands, love your wives, just as Christ loved the church and gave himself up for her to make her holy, cleansing her by the washing with water through the word, and to present her to himself as a radiant church, without stain or wrinkle or any other blemish, but holy and blameless. In this same way, husbands ought to love their wives as their own bodies. He who loves his wife loves himself. After all, no one ever hated his own body, but he feeds and cares for it, just as Christ does the church—for we are members of his body. "For this reason a man will leave his father and mother and be united to his wife, and the two will become one flesh." This is a profound mystery—but I am talking about Christ and the church. However, each one of you also must love his wife as he loves himself, and the wife must respect her husband.

EPHESIANS 5:21-33

I'm a little worried as I begin this chapter. I understand that there is great room for misunderstanding by persons of various opinions on many of the issues in this passage. Yet I am anxious to write this chapter. I have gained some insights into the whole concept of submission and roles. I want to share those insights.

I first became a Christian near the height of the "discipleship movement." This was a sometimes good and sometimes dangerous movement in which more mature Christians put younger Christians under their authority and told them how to live out their life of faith. Unlike mentoring, the movement deemphasized listening and advice-giving and tended toward giving orders.

As a child of the sixties, I didn't fit well into this type of movement. I remember the semester during college that a fellow whom I dearly love tried to "disciple" me. I simply refused to follow his orders. I was fired (as a volunteer) from the Christian organization where I worked under this fellow. I sincerely hold no grudge. But I can say that I learned something. I acquired a determination to never allow myself to be in that kind of situation again. And I made a further and more significant commitment. I vowed to never put anyone "under" my authority.

I will share about my relationship with God. I will share about my experiences. I will surely listen to another's story. I may even give some cheap advice. But I will never place a spiritual bit of slavery in someone else's mouth and tell that person that he or she must obey me.

So, several years ago, I came to the fifth chapter of Ephesians with my eyes wide open, and I saw some amazing things. This is not a passage that puts people "in their place." It is a passage that sets us free to excel in relationships.

Travel way back in time with me—to the first century. Our journey takes us to Ephesus in the heart of the Greco-Roman culture. The culture was male-dominated. Men predominantly ran the marketplace. Men had the power in society. For the most part, women were mere objects.

Here is what an object looked like. Women had no rights. They had no legal protection if divorced—and not a shred of social welfare coverage if put out of a home. Women were given and taken in marriage. They had no say in their relationships. No say about their bodies, their family size, their role inside the home. Men owned women. There was one Jewish prayer that said, "I thank you God that I am not a Gentile and I thank you even more that I am not a woman." In other words, women were placed in such a low status that they were even lower than a man who was not of God's family!

Our difficult passage in Ephesians opens with the words, "Submit to one another out of reverence for Christ." It doesn't say women submit to men or men submit to women or anything else—other than "submit to one another. . . ." The commandment here, the indication that one is a mature follower of Christ, is the practice of mutual submission.

Let's stay in the first century A.D. How did mutual submission look? What was the model? For women? For men? First of all, Paul encourages women to submit to their husbands as if the husband were Christ. The call is to a radical commitment of trust. Paul asks women to commit themselves fully to their husbands. Why was that important two thousand years ago? Because in that culture in which women were given to men in marriage without their input and placed under a man's roof and in his bed while at an age so young that, today, they could not even obtain a driver's license in the United States, it was hard for a woman to understand and respect her husband. Women felt like slaves. Like kitchen help. And they were.

You see, Paul is telling women in this passage, "Live the adventure of faith in Christ. Believe that God can make something out of your marriage. Don't resent the man who is your husband. Instead, give yourself to him. Take this social institution of cross-gender slavery and nullify it in Christ by creating an atmosphere wherein love can happen."

Men are told to love their wives as Christ loved the church. What did Christ do for the church? He gave himself—completely.

He did not come to this world with a show of strength and dominion or ownership; he came with a posture of servanthood and sacrifice. He treated the church with love. By placing the societal agenda of "owning" a woman on the back burner and replacing that with a genuine, nurturing love for another person, man is able to create a marriage of the quality that God intended in the beginning. After hearing or reading the apostle Paul, how could any man treat a woman as an object—particularly one given to him as a gift from God to be his wife?

Ephesians 5:21–33 restores marriages to the way God originally made them! Marriage is based upon mutual submission, mutual empowerment, and mutual nurturing. In the Fall of humankind recorded in Genesis 3:16, God expels Adam and Eve from their pristine Garden, and they are cursed for defying God's orders regarding how they should live. The curse God transmits to the woman is, "Your husband . . . shall rule over you."

Male chauvinism, marriage roles, and hierarchical interpersonal relationships are not a part of God's plan. They are part of the curse of the Fall! They are destructive remnants of sin's grip on our lives. However, the presence of Christ in our lives is the active power of God reversing that Garden curse. The presence of the Holy Spirit at the center of our being reverses the curse of the Fall. We are set free from oppressive patterns.

Not many days ago I sat in a beautiful candlelight service celebrating the birth of Jesus. We sang a familiar Christmas hymn, "Joy to the World," in which one verse says, "He comes to make his blessings known, far as the curse is found. . . ." Jesus Christ has come into the world launching a wave of curse-reversing. To be in partnership with God means to work for the health and healing of society at all levels, including redefining institutions and social mores so that they conform with the New Creation.

The apostle Paul added to the wave begun by Jesus as he wrote to the Ephesians. In a few short words ("submit to one another") he wipes out sexual discrimination of any sort and sets both genders free. Women are set free to bring all of who they are to marriage—to be full participants in the relationship. Men are set free to see to it that they give all of who they are to the relationship—and, frankly, are set free from being solely responsible for the happiness of their wives. Both partners can be a part of choosing what will make life work. Both partners explore what will make existence fulfilling.

As we read Ephesians 5:21–33 it becomes evident that Paul is making a first-century application of the principle of mutual submission. This truth is reinforced in Galatians 3:28, where Paul writes that in Christ there is neither male nor female. It is further evidenced in the ministry of Jesus as he makes close association with Mary Magdalene, the sisters Mary and Martha, and even his own mother.

Jesus often associated with women whom society would not defend. In John 4, it is a faith-building and dignity-restoring encounter with a woman who has failed in five marriages and is currently "shacking up" that seems to renew his mission after a long and trying journey. In John 8, it is an immoral woman caught in adultery whom Jesus defends—literally putting his life on the line as the Pharisees seek to label him a lawbreaker and put him to death.

In another passage of Scripture Jesus heals a woman with a hemorrhage—he touches someone considered ceremonially unclean and restores her health. Upon his resurrection, Jesus first appears to women. Jesus set women free. He did not give preference to anyone by gender.

Since mutual submission is the theme of this and the following two chapters, let's take some time to consider what mutual submission looks like in our current Western culture.

There is no room for chauvinism. Women and men are coequals in God's kingdom and coequals in society. Let me add that while this statement refers to a biblical injunction against male chauvinism, it is also a biblical injunction against angry feminism. What plays to one gender must also play for the other. There is no biblical basis in Ephesians 5 for entitlement as a result of past injustices, either.

As followers of Christ, we have no time to spend making up for past grievances. Jesus began a wave of justice. We ride it together into the future—male and female. I have seen beautiful things happen when men and women have been allowed to be themselves, free of gender roles.

Also implicit in the retraction of chauvinism is the abolition of role distinctions. Remembering the context of mutual submission, women who are gifted for work in the marketplace should be free to pursue that kind of work. Men who are nurturers and wish to work in the home (I know a number) ought to utilize their gifts and stay home.

Further, the "chain of command" taught in so many Christian discipleship courses is not an acceptable model. It is a reflection of the Fall, not the New Creation. Martin Luther staged the beginning of the Reformation. He demanded that Reformed churches place the Bible and the sacraments between the pastor and the parishioner. He was intentionally declaring that in Christ there is no chain of command. Christ is in command. Each of us has access to Christ directly, without intermediaries.

So it is in social institutions, particularly Christian organizations. Men and women are both subject to Christ alone, and accountable in community to each other as coequals. Here is the true "chain of command": Jesus Christ to individuals—individuals responding to Jesus Christ. Leaders and support groups exist only to reinforce this true chain of command. Any other behavior is a presumptuous supplanting of authority.

I think of a dear friend who is a great Christian educator. She has all the gifts and training that it takes to be an effective administrator and teacher in the church setting. She has a strong educational background and years of experience in the public schools. I am always amazed when she stands up to teach a biblical lesson. When my friend shows up to teach, this old boy has his pen out and is stealing material for his next lesson on that passage. I delight in seeing my friend succeed. It hasn't always been this way for her.

A number of years ago, she and her husband were embroiled in a system where he had to be the boss and she had to submit to his wishes. He alone could be the "front" person in the family. As her gifts emerged, it became evident that his gifts for ministry were not "up-front" gifts, but rather gifts of service, encouragement, and compassion. This put their marriage in a tailspin. The marriage was extremely threatened for a short time. But they were both willing to let God lead them—and the result was a woman set free to be what God meant her to be and a man set free to not have to try and be what he was not.

The end result was a beautiful mutuality. She did not need redress for the years of oppression. He did not need a "medal" since he was willing to change. They each followed Christ boldly and wound up in a great place!

Mutual submission is rooted in God's grace. Only as we experience the depths of God's love for us, as we experience forgiveness and the present power of the Holy Spirit in our lives, can we bring those God-given resources to our relationships. Jesus Christ is our model of submission and servanthood. The Spirit is our source of strength to live relationships that honor Christ. Grace in relationships means being more willing to give oneself than to claim rights.

Grace in relationships means being willing to believe in the other for the long haul. Grace in relationships means to judge one's own motives and behavior very carefully while assuming that the other is operating with the best intentions.

I have to admit that this is a hard area for me. I am a type A person. I go at a fast pace. When I finally slow down, relax, and reflect, I don't want anyone bothering me. Often, when I am in this hermit mode and get interrupted by my wife or daughter, I am quick to feel sabotaged, as if my rights are violated—and for the worst reasons. It's hard to bring grace to our relationships and practice mutual submission. I want to be in control. I want to hold the deck and to deal the cards I want when I want.

Leadership is expressed when males and females work together equally. The best research now being done on the workplace is saying that men and women speak in different voices. Our genetics, our socialization, and our temperaments all lead us to see things differently. The best example I have heard of this differentiation in "voices" comes from an elementary school playground.

When boys play baseball, most will stay long and argue exuberantly over rules interpretations or who has the right to bat in which order. The boys will fight and fight—verbally and sometimes physically—to reach resolution.

Over on the other side of the playground, a group of girls playing tetherball has a similar difficulty in resolving who is where and why. The girls one by one leave the game and go off to another activity. Why? Because where resolution of "right facts" in community was key to the boys, preservation of "right relationships" in community was critical to the girls. Who is right? Both voices—male and female.

A coed baseball game, four-square game—or leadership team in a church or business office—would look quite different as both male and female voices would receive consideration.

In relationships we must look at ourselves first. The biblical model for improved human relationships appears to be based upon self-examination rather than criticism of the other party. That means that when I am having a problem in my marriage, it is first my problem. Now, I am not setting up a scenario for codependency here. I am not denying that there may be things about each of us in a marriage relationship that are destructive to the well-being of the other.

Some relationships are sick because one or both parties are unhealthy spiritually and psychologically. Sometimes those sick relationships have to be dealt with in head-on confrontation, through therapy, or, in the case of abuse, perhaps even by separation. What

I am saying is that healthy self-examination is the first step of intervention in moving toward mutual submission.

The greatest gift we give to each other is communication. That means that marriage becomes a place where it is safe to say who we are and how we are feeling. Mutual submission carries with it an implicit demand that each of us be willing to probe the other for how we are feeling and reveal the secrets of our hearts to one another.

I remember the first time I told Nancy that I wasn't particularly excited about where our marriage was. We had been through a two-year period of changing jobs, starting businesses, having a child, reworking our finances, and running madly in all directions. Each of us felt far from the other. We felt lost. We weren't sure how much we liked our lives.

When I said I wasn't liking our marriage at the moment, Nancy was set free to share her own dissatisfaction. And in the end she gave me a great gift. She said, "Now that we agree there are things we are concerned and frustrated about, we can start to work on them." Out of our mutual weakness came communication that strengthened our relationship.

If I had felt that I needed to be in charge around the home and marriage, I would have just given out a list of demands. If she had felt that she just needed to be submissive, she would have taken my offering of discontent as a one-way communication and would have had to live with her feelings buried inside. Our relationship would have been robbed of a chance to grow.

Thank God for mutuality.

14 Kids Count

Children, obey your parents in the Lord, for this
is right. "Honor your father and mother"—
which is the first commandment with a
promise—"that it may go well with you and that
you may enjoy long life on the earth." Fathers,
do not exasperate your children; instead, bring
them up in the training and instruction of the
Lord.

EPHESIANS 6:1-4

It all happened during Monday night football. Guess where I
was? I was on the couch in front of the television sprawled out
like a sunbathing sea lion. My daughter, Rachel, age four, was
tearing around the living room nursing Mickey Mouse dolls, coloring, jumping, practicing her ballet, and spelling her name aloud.
I enjoy that. But Rachel has a way of getting Daddy's attention
when the old boy is immersed in some good smash-face football.
She stands between me and the television and says, "Daddy!"

On this particular evening, I had warned her on several occasions that she was threatening to shorten her life span if the screen-
blocking behavior continued, but the message didn't sink in.
Finally Dad lost it. (I know what you're thinking. You want your
money back from buying this book because the author is an un-
caring couch-potato dweeb.)

I raised my voice and said, "Rachel! Knock it off! I am not enjoying your attention-getting scheme here." My little angel stomped down the hall crying mournfully, "You hurt my feelings. You don't like me anymore." Later that night when I went to pray with her and tuck her into bed, I decided to have a chat. I said, "Rachel, you know I am crazy in love with you, but I don't like it when you clamor too much for attention (even though you learned it from me). So, I had to let you know you were out of line. Do you understand?"

"Yeah," said Rachel.

"Are we okay with each other?" I asked.

Rachel looked at me, "Hey, we're still living together, aren't we?"

I almost fell off the bed. What a profound understanding of our relationship. Rachel understands our long-term commitment to each other and the fact that conflict has a beginning and an end. She was communicating as a very mature person. She does that often. I like it.

Our little conversation helped me to understand better what the apostle Paul means in Ephesians 6:1–4 when he asks for children to obey and parents not to provoke. Rachel was willing to obey my wish for her to settle down and quit seeking attention, even though it hurt her. I found myself quite concerned that she understand that I interacted with her as one person to another over a matter of sharing space in the home. I blow it so often that I really marveled when I followed the biblical model and it worked.

The biblical text we are examining in this chapter is related to the previous chapter's discussion of men's and women's roles. It too falls under the headline of Ephesians 5:21, "Submit to one another out of reverence for Christ." There is mutual submission in our relationships with our kids. It starts at the cradle and becomes more and more critical as they become increasingly capable of making their own wise choices and functioning as adults. One day, the mutuality will be a parity and my little Rachel will be a grown woman— and I hope will be among my two or three best friends on this planet.

First, let me state that Ephesians 6:1–4 has often been used as a tool for thumping kids into obedience and making them feel guilty for having minds of their own. I think such an interpretation is completely opposite to what Paul intended.

Next, let me ask you, who has the most responsibility for making mutuality happen, a little person or a grown-up? Obviously, the grown-up. The message here is first and foremost for us parents. We can help our kids become healthy and well-adjusted adults by giving them a sense of self-esteem. We need to let kids know that they matter, that their ideas and feelings are real and worthy of respect.

On the other side, we need to let our children know that life has limits and that there are principles for making it through this life. One of those principles is respecting voices of authority, responding to disciplinary situations by learning from them and looking beyond our own wants, experiences, and feelings to the wants, feelings, and experiences of others. This is how we are enriched. This is how we grow.

Interestingly, Paul borrows from the Ten Commandments, "Honor your father and mother. . . ." Recent study of the ancient Hebrew text of this passage from Exodus, combined with cultural studies, indicates that it was probably a command for mid-life adults to care for their aging parents. I don't think that means that children shouldn't honor, obey, and learn from their parents, but it creates a beautiful picture of a cycle of mutual submission and interdependence from the cradle to the grave.

Imagine, I nurture my child and help her develop her potential. Later in life as I have reached my peak and gone beyond it, there will be a relationship that carries with it the love, respect, and interdependence that will perhaps allow her to nurture me. With every cut and scrape I doctor, every hard lesson I have to teach, I keep that in mind, knowing that perhaps someday my turn will come.

At the same time, I am mindful of the fact that my parents nurtured me. They provided a great home, a good education, and my first car. We had all the good and bad times that families experience. Now the time is approaching for me to be able to return to my own parents some of the nurture that they lavished on me when I was young.

This cycle of interdependency between persons explains why Paul goes on to finish this passage with a warning for parents, "Fathers [parents], do not exasperate your children." Again, Paul is emphasizing that as we approach our children, we are not dealing with objects, not raising cattle or building automatons. Rather, we are engaging in a human relationship. A primary relationship. A relationship that will forever shape how both parent and child deal with each other and all other relationships.

A few years ago I spoke at a church. I was talking about being discerning and mentioned how critical "teachable moments" in life can be. I discussed how, as we parents encounter our children in disciplinary or teaching situations, we are under a tremendous pressure to do the right thing because once we act, we cannot take back our action even though forgiveness, apologies, and reconciliation can take place down the road. The whole idea of becoming discerning is that we develop skills and intuition that allow us to do it right the first time when we are on the spot.

Well, many people liked the sermon. Some parents shared from their experience how right they thought I was. That always feels good. But a moment later a man, probably in his sixties, walked up to me and let me have it. He said that I never held the kids responsible. He said that kids are such a mess because they are bad kids, not because they have bad parents, or parents who are not skillful enough at their job of parenting.

I felt compassion for this distraught man. He clearly seemed to be experiencing deep pain regarding his own family situation. He didn't let up on me. I was forced to respond to his questions.

Gently, I pointed out to him that of the thirteen hundred or so people in the church, only a small handful were not parental-aged adults. Second, I noted that if we play it right, our children spend most of the years that they are with us in our homes as the "reactors." That is, parents are the prime movers in the relationship between a big person and a little person. Finally, I pointed out that none of what I said means that anybody is capable of being a perfect parent or a perfect child and that we all make mistakes along the way, but that I was going to make the healthiness of my relationship with my daughter my responsibility. Responding to my wisdom, insights, and people-winning communication skills, the man told me I was full of meadow muffins and left the immediate area.

In spite of my miserable failure with this well-meaning church attender, I believe these points are valid. The first is that Paul is writing, inspired by the Holy Spirit, to big people—adults, parents. He's not first and foremost writing to kids. So, let's own the fact that we adults are the target audience.

Second, Paul's encouragement to relate to children so that they mature in the training and instruction of the Lord is, I believe, a clear indication that parents are to be "actors," not "reactors," in the relationship. We can spend a lot of time being negative and reacting parents rather than nurturing adult friends who bring young people along the path of life.

Third, the mutual submission described by Paul leads us to allow lots of grace into the relationship between parents and children. I know that as the years go by, I will inflict some emotional and spiritual wounds on Rachel. I jokingly say I have two investment accounts with her name on them—one is the college tuition fund and the other is the counseling/therapy fund. Most people who know me and my quirks are urging me to place heavy emphasis on the therapy fund.

I make this joke in some seriousness. Someday my children may need loving friends, extended family, a pastor, or a therapist to help them work through certain views of the world and relationship styles that I in my control, neglect, protectiveness, or permissiveness have passed along to my children.

I know that my kids will need to make a choice someday. Either they will choose to forgive me my shortcomings, realize that I did my best, and accept me, or they will have to hold grudges and cut me out of their lives. That will be their choice. Likewise, I will no doubt have some baggage. I will need to unload it and go on loving or become a spiritual and emotional wreck. So I am trying to learn to live in grace and forgiveness now on the little day-to-day things.

I am learning slowly to cry and tell my child, "Dad is sorry. I was dead wrong. Will you forgive me?" I have also learned to hear "I'm sorry, Dad" in Rachel's hugs and kisses or other forms of reconnecting the relationship after a difficult encounter between us.

I'll never forget the night recently when I heard Rachel pounding her feet on the floor and I was certain she was cursing, "Damn, damn, damn!" I marched into the hallway where she was and said, "We don't talk like that here, young lady. Go to your room right now." She exploded into a convulsing cry and went to her room for the required time-out. She was so beside herself that Nancy went in to visit her.

It turns out that she had been watching a children's video and was doing a dance that included the foot pounding and the words "Stamp, Stamp, Stamp." Boy, did I feel like a heel. I went to a heartbroken little girl and begged for her forgiveness in tears.

I learned from this. It was my first official "Dad is a moron" apology. And do you know what? It felt good afterwards. I think I can get used to a mutually nurturing relationship in which I don't always have to be right!

Some final thoughts:

1. Kids are people. They deserve respect. If you speak to kids like people and treat them like people, they will respond and communicate like people. It's wonderful.

2. Respect is earned. Parents should be respected. But respect is not conveyed or bestowed upon someone. It is earned the old-fashioned way by listening, caring, spending time with and imparting

leadership to children. Leadership is not management. Leadership implies giving children a vision of what life can be. Leadership means teaching, explaining, and reteaching core values as means of attaining a vision for life. Such behavior wins respect.

3. Harsh parenting develops harsh children. Some discipline must be done with intensity and emotion, but that is the exception. Children who make mistakes deserve to be treated the same way we would nurture a good friend embroiled in the consequences of a major mistake or problem. Studies show that harsh parenting of any form often leads to violent behaviors in children.

4. Good relationships produce good memories. We need to be memory makers with our children. We can turn ordinary circumstances into learning experiences that reinforce core values. We can also turn them into lifelong memories. We teach in our house that God answers prayers. When we came upon a serious car wreck, Nancy and Rachel prayed, while a squeamish dad went to try and help the man who was trapped in his car. Later, we found out that the man was all right. Rachel said, "Jesus helped him." She has on a number of occasions recounted that situation to me. She knows that bad things happen. But she believes in God's care and the power of prayer. She has a living memory of God's active love.

15 Mutual Empowerment

Slaves, obey your earthly masters with respect
and fear, and with sincerity of heart, just as you
would obey Christ. Obey them not only to win
their favor when their eye is on you, but like
slaves of Christ, doing the will of God from your
heart. Serve wholeheartedly, as if you were serving the Lord, not men, because you know that
the Lord will reward everyone for whatever good
he does, whether he is slave or free. And masters,
treat your slaves in the same way. Do not
threaten them, since you know that he who is
both their Master and yours is in heaven, and
there is no favoritism with him.

EPHESIANS 6:5-9

It was an absolute stress day. We were taping a television special. I was the producer. Frustrated with the disorganization of
our band and choral group, I reprimanded them for not being
on top of things. "Time's wasting, money's burning," I told them,
adding that they were unprepared and inattentive. One of the choir
members, a former college fullback, stormed up to me. I thought he
was going to punch out my lights. Instead, he punched verbally, "I
quit. You treat people like meat. I'm not your slave." Then he left.

I was devastated. I knew that I had been very wrong. I went into
the studio, called everyone together, and apologized profusely. I

even offered to quit. In my moment of failure and vulnerability, the performers forgave me. The show went on—and it came off very well. I learned a big lesson that day about how not to lead others. Slaves and masters—the biblical terms are not found in our most current management and sociology texts! How can such ancient words representing an evil and abolished institution speak to those of us zooming toward the twenty-first century? Let's examine the text carefully and bring it into our modern era.

First, note that, culturally, Paul does not speak out about the evils of slavery. What he does is redefine the institution, just as he redefined the intent for men and women in marriage relationships in Ephesians 5:21–33. Here Paul insists that those who are slaves perform their life's work as if they were working for Christ himself. Similarly, Paul entreats masters to relate to their slaves as if they were Christ himself.

Unfortunately, this scripture was used to validate the institution of slavery for many years right here in America. It was also the text for sermons affirming a "kinder and gentler" form of slavery. Actually, though, the heart of the text calls for the abolition of slavery. How could anyone own other people, force them to work long hours, keep them in squalor, and restrain them with chains and yet claim to be treating them as if they were Christ? It would be impossible for Christians to put Jesus Christ the Lord in leg shackles and force him into service for their benefit. In essence, Paul is saying that slavery cannot work.

So, just as chauvinism and negative parenting are eliminated by Ephesians 5:21–6:9, slavery is eliminated. Each negative social pattern, as I explained earlier, has been replaced by a higher law of Love. Each higher principle is a reversal of the Fall and aeons of sin. The specific form of love demonstrated in this section of Ephesians is mutual submission. Chauvinism gives way to a shared relationship between men and women; negative parenting gives way to active parenting that treats children as people; and, finally, slavery gives way to an open marketplace where all persons are equal and relate to one another by choice for mutual empowerment and financial gain.

By the way, I am convinced that if you believe that Ephesians 5:22–33 justifies hierarchical roles in marriage, then you also have to believe in strong parental rule over children and the elimination of children's rights. And you also have to believe in slavery. People who argue about this long section of scripture cannot deny that the passage is a single unit expressing a single theme. If that is so, consistency in interpretation is essential. If you do not believe that slavery is legitimate, then Ephesians 5:21–6:9 leaves no room for abusive parenting or chauvinism.

With this introduction, I would like to move to what appear to be the two specific principles Paul is communicating to those of us who seek to be partners with God in our social relationships.

The first principle is that people who find themselves in subordinate or disprivileged roles are to somehow order their lives so that they are playing to a new audience. That audience is Jesus Christ. The point here is that even when we are not in total control of our social circumstances, we are supposed to work wholeheartedly to be productive. This is a hard statement. I admit that I feel trapped by it. You see, I find in myself a good deal of the blood of America's founding fathers. I tend to feel that if you don't like the system or the deal you're getting, you go on strike or revolt. You create a new order.

I am not sure that the apostle Paul's encouragement to work wholeheartedly as if working for Christ extends to abusive situations. I am sure that this passage of scripture tempers our desire to lash out, to be bitter, angry, and resentful. It reminds us to whom we will finally have to answer for where we have spent the energy of our lives. We will answer to Jesus Christ.

I have to believe that this passage must have spoken strongly to freedom fighters like Martin Luther King, Jr. It probably motivated him to say "I have a dream . . ." rather than "I have a bomb. . . ."

Fortunately, most of us, even though we feel disenfranchised or unempowered, will not face moral struggles of such global size as the civil rights movement. Our battles will be at Apple Computer, Boeing Aerospace, Merrill Lynch, Central High School, and the other places where we spend our days working both for money and for a sense of self-worth. Some of those days will be hard. Sometimes the organizations we work for or a specific supervisor rob us of earning potential that we believe we have coming—or even more frequently rob us of our self-worth. Paul's answer to those situations is this: while you are where you are, work whole-heartedly, as if you were working for Jesus Christ. Be a person who makes a difference. If you cannot do that any longer, do yourself and the organization a favor and move on.

I worked for eight years at a very large broadcasting company. I loved my job, the people, and the company—at least for the first three years. The last five years were a disappointment. Often I felt like I was, as a friend says, the "live chick being put under a dead hen." I worked for a large number of questionably competent bosses at several levels of the company. My co-workers and I marveled at the company's lack of understanding of what it would take for our division to be a winner.

The result was a decline in my attitude toward work. I was no longer working as if for Christ. I was no longer striving for excellence. I wasn't growing professionally. I became more interested in collecting paychecks and pay raises than in seeing the company prosper. I began to withhold time at work. I just went through the motions. I was dying to be laid off and collect a good severance from a company I once loved but now only tolerated. I rejoiced when the day came that the station laid off thirty people and I got to be one of them.

Over a period of months after leaving, I realized what had happened. I had compromised my integrity. I lost my passion for work. I was not working as if for Christ. Neither was I being of any benefit to an already struggling company. I was doing what NFL football coach Chuck Knox calls "the loser's lament." I bought into a loser's mentality and, in doing so, was actually destroying myself and hurting the company. Let me sum that up: I was being counterproductive to God's re-creation of the world.

Paul's second point is that people who do hold positions of power and influence have a responsibility to those who do not have power. They have a responsibility to use power to enable, empower, and nurture others. Using power to control, demean, and intimidate others is not acceptable partnership with God.

Let me tell another story about an experience in the broadcast business. One of the bosses of questionable competence that I mentioned earlier was hired to run the operations of the station. He was surly, coercive, and a poor communicator. Further, he didn't seem to genuinely care about anyone.

One day, the staff had really put itself out covering a winter storm. When he showed up for work at a comfortable ten o'clock in the morning, we had questions for him relating to our on-air broadcasts. I was sent to ask him what to do. He told me he didn't want to talk to me or anybody else. It was early in the morning and he just wanted to be left alone. He walked into the company cafeteria—literally turning his back on me. I said, "Those kind of communication skills are going to come back to bite you in the butt!" Then I left for my office.

Within three months I had about six such encounters with this guy, plus I had been forced to do job assignments I was never consulted about. He didn't last long at the radio station. He was gone in less than a hundred days from his hiring. He violated all the laws of power and himself became powerless.

I think that is why we who are given authority must wield it carefully. We are just one breath away from being made powerless. If we attempt to be fair and just, then we can expect a better longevity in our positions of power.

At this juncture let's take a look at some specific areas in the marketplace wherein Paul's discussion about slaves and masters has current application:

In the workplace. I have discussed the area of work quite a bit. Let me reiterate that mutuality begins at the top. Those who have power should be the first to share it—to give it away. Second, those who are not empowered should not seek power for its own sake, but rather power to make a difference—to be a force for good.

One of my favorite tests to see if people live this passage in Ephesians at their place of work is to observe how people treat those at work to whom they don't *have* to be nice. Most of us try to stroke bosses or key co-workers. But how do we treat the person from the mail room, or the temporary who is answering phones at the front desk?

I cannot help but remember a shocking story about a famous NFL football star in my hometown. He was renowned for his verbal Christianity. Hardly a press interview went by with me or someone else when he didn't mention God in some way or another. One day, I was having coffee in the team's press room when one of the team's college interns came into the room looking very glum. I liked this fellow immensely, so I sat by him and asked what was up. He told me how for an entire season, from early July until November, he had been verbally abused, humiliated, and walked on by the famous Christian player. The young fellow was a Christian, too. He wanted to know how to handle the situation. I encouraged him to realize that the problem was not his and do the best he could until the internship ended. I later found out through other sources that the football star had done this through the years to anyone whom he didn't have to be nice to. His stock really dropped in my eyes.

A key barometer for all of us is, how do we treat the people we don't have to be nice to?

Between various socioeconomic groups. Tragically, our society is not a place where all persons experience the same level of prosperity. Because of race, family money, and other factors, some of us have gotten privileged places in our society where we can earn money and recognition. Others, equally gifted, are left unempowered. They are trapped in poverty. They are the disprivileged of our world.

Both privileged and disprivileged have their own sets of baggage to deal with. For the privileged, it is our duty to realize that we are blessed. Our good position has not been all our own doing—in fact, some of it has been accumulated at the expense of the disprivileged. Paul's message to people who are empowered economically is to be compassionate, generous, and accepting of those who have been less fortunate.

For those of us who have struggled at a lower socioeconomic level, there is an equal biblical responsibility: the responsibility to live our lives for Christ and to do all we can to improve our situation, improve our society, and empower those around us the best we are able.

I loved the story I saw on a television documentary about a small group of women in a housing project in Chicago. They were poor. They were part of the social-welfare system. But they were holders of a deep Christian faith and persons who wanted to make a difference. They decided to start at home. They would no longer lash out at the housing authorities and the system. They committed themselves to making things better.

They began a community-improvement campaign in this low-income housing development where even cabs wouldn't enter. They struggled to end drug dealing, violence, intimidation, gang activity, and many other terrible problems that had made this project one of the scariest places in all of America. They beautified the buildings and the grounds of this place that even the police had abandoned.

Beginning with just two or three persons and a vision for how to make their faith relevant and their world a better place, these women took a situation of nonpower and not only became powerful but became powerful enablers of others. They practiced transformative leadership from the grass-roots level. Working as if we are working for Christ can change what appears to be a hopeless and powerless life situation into a New Creation.

In the church. Most of our churches are run by pastors and/or small groups of powerful people. The average person is given little say in the operation of the church. The people are usually left to "like it or lump it." Judging by the state of the Protestant church in America, particularly mainline churches, most have lumped it. God is alive and well, but the church is dying because the power brokers won't let go.

Church boards (substitute any name for a ruling body) have traditionally figured that they know more about people's needs and more about what legitimate ministry consists of than the people in the church. They won't admit this openly, but they say it by their behavior.

That is antithetical to the model of Ephesians 6:5–9. The question people in positions of power in the church should be asking is, "How can I help make your dreams for ministry come true? What can I do to help?" A friend of mine calls this the blank-check policy. You have an idea, we have a blank check to give you the resources to get it done.

Many of us have been hurt by the church at one time or another. I sure have. I counsel quite a few people who are ready to leave the church or have left—because they felt caught in the gears of a power mechanism that chewed them up and spit them out.

The apostle Paul has a message for those of us who have been victims of church power. We have to realize that we aren't a part of the church to pursue some agenda of our own making (power, self-esteem, influence, popularity, and so on). Rather, we are a part of the church to work for Christ and with Christ. That means we can be free to pursue creative service ideas and positive interpersonal relationships even if we do get creamed when we try to be a part of the official power system. We can work as though we are working for Christ and do so outside the sphere of the organizational system.

By this I mean be a part of Bible studies or other small-group fellowships, have influence among a peer group that can use your gifts and talents. I am reminded of the movie *War Games,* in which some young kids hack a government computer and set off a simulated thermonuclear war that moves within inches of becoming a real world war. In the end, one of the teenagers and a scientist who invented the simulated war game for the government try to beat the computer at its game and end the threat of war. In a final move, they ask the computer how to win. The computer answers, "The only way to win is not to play the game."

What an insight. I think that is at the heart of what Paul is telling us in Ephesians 6:5–9. Whether we are empowered or disempowered in our current situation, we can choose not to play the power game.

In interpersonal relationships. Paul advises people with power not to treat anyone with partiality. He says this because he understands that God is impartial and does not play favorites.

This is a hard saying for me. I am so often drawn to people who are just like me. I like people who reflect my best attributes and reinforce me with their presence. Better yet, I like people who possess fame or other attributes that I lack. Those are the people that I tend to believe can really round out my life and make me somebody.

God's message to us through Paul is that this sort of behavior is counterproductive. We should relate to people based upon each person's unique worth in God's sight—not based upon our country club membership-selection-committee mentalities.

I am not a physically coordinated person. I am a klutz. I do a five-minute car headlight change in one hour flat. No wonder I have always had a problem relating to the blue-collar folks of this world. It's hard for me to comprehend someone enjoying yard work, auto mechanics projects, or home remodeling. Therefore, out of my own lack of self-esteem in the "blue-collar" area of life, I tend to shy away from people with that orientation. God tells me through Ephesians 6:5–9 that my behavior is preferential treatment. I prefer "my kind" of people—and tend to block others out. I need to grow.

Ephesians 6:5–9 is a very positive and very encouraging passage. In it, God gives us a glimpse of what social or working relationships can be like if we learn to view every person as if he or she were Christ. The phrase "as if they were Christ" really boils down to treating people with dignity, treating them with respect as unique and unrepeatable gifts from God to the world. Frankly, if we treat people like that, they will respond positively and we will find that our lives are making a difference.

Mutual submission is a life-style that begins deep in the center of our lives as the Holy Spirit tells us who we are and brings the incredible worth of others to our consciousness. Mutual submission is a great gift to us and to the world. Mutual submission works in all phases of life.

PART
FIVE

Introduction

So it is with our lives. We each have a personal history full of ups and downs. We have individual strengths and weaknesses. In the midst of who we are and all that is going on around us, God desires to equip us to successfully play out our part in the drama of God's re-creation.

This book has reiterated the notion that all of us desire to be connected with the true purpose of life. The apostle Paul has argued—and I have interpreted his argument—that such purpose is found in a deep and transforming relationship with God through Jesus Christ. We have discussed the nature of God's power in human lives, God's intent for relationships, ethics, and even societal roles. We have seen that God wants our relationship with him to make a difference in all of life. Deep in our hearts, we want to be counted. We want to make a difference.

Andy Warhol has said that in our world everybody gets to be famous for fifteen minutes. We all have a moment of glory as we flash across the television, newspaper, silver screen, magazine, book, or radio program. Well, God's design for things is different from Warhol's. God calls us to a life of continuous and meaningful engagements with the world throughout our years. Our impact is not measured by the visibility of our "fifteen minutes of fame," but by the eternal value of the ripples that proceed outward from each of our actions. God invites us to engage our world in a life-long process in which, whether observed or unobserved, we are partners with him in being change agents. Armed with God's resources of faith, salvation, Scripture, hope, and passion, we can participate in the re-creation of God's world and have incredible impact.

16 Dress for Success

Finally, be strong in the Lord and in his mighty power. Put on the full armor of God so that you can take your stand against the devil's schemes. For our struggle is not against flesh and blood, but against the rulers, against the authorities, against the powers of this dark world and against the spiritual forces of evil in the heavenly realms. Therefore put on the full armor of God, so that when the day of evil comes, you may be able to stand your ground, and after you have done everything, to stand. Stand firm then, with the belt of truth buckled around your waist, with the breastplate of righteousness in place, and with your feet fitted with the readiness that comes from the gospel of peace. In addition to all this, take up the shield of faith, with which you can extinguish all the flaming arrows of the evil one. Take the helmet of salvation and the sword of the Spirit, which is the word of God. And pray in the Spirit on all occasions with all kinds of prayers and requests. With this in mind, be alert and always keep on praying for all the saints.

EPHESIANS 6:10–18

I recently overheard a conversation between two people concerning a magazine article about a man who went into a chicken factory. He wound up talking to the chicken sexer, whose job it was to look at chickens to see what sex they were.

A short time later, the same man went to a leather factory. He met a man who was grading hides to decide where the hides went. The visitor asked if it was the worker's job to segregate good hides from bad hides. The worker said that was not his job at all. He noted that these were all the best hides. It was his job to sort through them and determine what they were to be made into. Some are better for leather coats and some are better for purses.

The factory visitor concluded that one of the difficult things we face as Christians is that we would like to live in a world where chicken sexers are needed. Grade a chicken to see if it is a girl or boy and that determines the way to ship it. But the reality is that we live in a more complex world, one more like that of the leather hide sorter. We have to choose between not just what is good and better, but what everything is best used for.

The discernment that we must have as God's people in this world is very difficult to come by. We are surrounded by the media, including Christian radio and television stations, teaching us to be chicken sexers: "this is right and this is wrong." I think Ephesians 6:10–18 helps us understand what we face in our world.

Having grown up in the sixties I find it difficult to relate to war-type analogies. Yet Paul has chosen warfare armor. So let's try and work with what's in the text. Because I have trouble with this imagery and maybe you do too, let's ask some questions.

First, what is the war? It is a battle between God's forces for re-creation and everything that resists God's restorative plans. Where is the war? We fight on a couple of different fronts. All of us fight on spiritual fronts at the internal level. That's the warfare we experience at night when we can't fall asleep, or in the morning when we wake up and wish we didn't have to. That's the conflict we fight on the inside of us against pride, greed, ambition, depression, fear, anxiety, and stress.

On another front, the universe is a war zone. There is an external spiritual battle. Here is a list of things with which we are at war: apartheid, racism, homelessness, the growing rich-poor gap in America, inadequate education, pornography, pollution, mental illness, child abuse, runaways, teen pregnancy, drugs, suicide, unethical business activity, and deadness in the church, just to name a few.

More questions: Who is the enemy? What are the authorities, rulers, and principalities of which Paul writes? Many have probably read this passage over the years and spiritualized it. We view evil powers as the devil and all his bad guys. Actually, when you read this in the Greek it refers to world systems. The devil is the author of the evil in the world, but most of the evil is created by the labor of human beings with systems and institutions that we have established. "Evil" is everything that opposes God in the New Creation that is taking place in Christ. Evil comes in various shapes.

Let's look at types of evil. First, there is the intentional evil of persons such as Hitler and other agents of the Holocaust. Some people would say that certain current world leaders have brought intentional evil into the world.

The second type of evil is misdirected. Our welfare system was conceived with the best intentions, yet many leading social scientists point to this system as oppressive. Claims can be made that the welfare system traps people into a form of economic slavery. There is nothing wrong with helping people in need, but the system goes wrong when generations of people are raised to believe that this subsistence form of living is all there is to life. The system's long-term results are evil. The result of the system is a form of social evil, created not by malicious intentions but by misdirected good intentions.

A third aspect of evil is ignorance. In the nineteenth century the death rate for women having babies was climbing toward thirty percent. A woman had a one-in-three chance of not coming out of the delivery room alive. The problem was infection. A doctor in the mid-nineteenth century discovered that if you washed your hands and instruments with bleach, the death rate dropped dramatically. He announced his research findings, but his colleagues scoffed at him. He was laughed at until the day he died. Then about forty years later other people discovered that if instruments were sterilized more women lived past delivery. Sterilization of surgical tools became the norm. But that didn't come until after the evil of ignorance had caused innumerable deaths. The struggle with evil is not easy. Paul says we struggle with powers and principalities. The word *struggle* is translated as "wrestle." It seems impossible to keep our hands clean when we wrestle with the world.

The chaplain of the United States Senate, Richard Halverson, tells a sad story. He got a letter from someone who had devised an evangelism system that worked through a computer hooked up to a telephone. It called people up and told them the gospel over the phone. If they wanted to respond they could push "1" on their phone keypad, and they would get literature in the mail. He concluded in the letter that the great thing about this system is that you don't get mixed up in people's lives and in their sin.

I've got news for this inventor: real spiritual warfare is exactly the opposite. To be God's people and really live out our faith means to be tangled up in the evil itself, to wrestle with it.

By the way, we should never underestimate our enemy. I think sometimes we take the devil too lightly and underestimate the forces of evil in this world. We need to be well armed to survive encounters with evil.

Paul encourages us to "put on the full armor of God." "Full," in Greek, means "complete." What is interesting is that Paul doesn't mention every type of armor that a Roman soldier wore. He uses strategic pieces very symbolically. One of the things about the full armor of God is that God has given us all the resources we need, not only to deal with the evil in our own lives but to deal with the evil in our society. Armor prepares us to "stand." "Stand" means "to hold the position." When Christians hold a position we find it is not easy. It can cost a lot to fight in the world.

Mark Hatfield, a U.S. senator from Oregon, said of the Vietnam War, "This is an evil war. We should not be fighting it." When we started shuttle diplomacy with the Soviets, he backed Mr. Kissinger's efforts. He also once made a statement to Congress that the people of the Soviet Union are children of God, just like us. He ostracized himself from his party and probably gave up any chance of becoming president of the United States.

I make no pointed statement here. I am simply saying that Hatfield took a stand against the prevailing wind of the time. We look back twenty years later and realize that Vietnam wasn't a great war any way you look at it, and we are starting to view the Soviet people as children of God.

Standing can have a cost. We can even be labeled as evil for fighting evil. Jesus was accused of being from the devil when he healed people on the Sabbath. Sometimes our "stand" doesn't make sense until a generation or two after our time. But right is right—and as Christians we have been equipped by God to stand. We have tremendous resources for "staying power" in the core of our lives.

Most of us recall our mothers saying to us on the way out the door, "Don't forget your coat or you'll catch cold." What I think Paul is saying when he tells us to "put on the armor" is, "Don't forget the armor or you could catch hell." Don't walk out the door without the resources that God has given you to make your life work. This is serious business. Let's check out the wardrobe.

The belt of truth. The belt on a Roman soldier held everything together. The truth in Paul's thinking is a person, Christ. Beyond that, truth is an intellectual thing, knowing what's right.

On a recent trip to Los Angeles I was listening to Dr. Demento, an infamous local radio personality. He was playing a song called "The Guru Rap." "G-U-R-U, gee you are you." One of the lines of this song was, "Mental floss each day. It helps prevent truth decay."

As Christians, we often fail to "mental floss"—we don't think things through. We probably need to analyze our world more carefully. We have to look at things from God's eternal perspective.

We have to begin to think. We need to use a little mental floss: know the Scriptures; know the issues and how to back them up with Scripture.

I was talking to a friend recently who said that he doesn't read the newspaper. When I asked him why, he said it was because he was a Christian. Reading the newspaper brings him down and he can't handle it. That's the opposite of where Christians should live their lives. We need to be informed.

The breastplate of righteousness. This was considered heart protection. It was mainly used to protect the soldier from being run through the heart by a spear or arrow. Heart protection is one of the things we so often lack as we try to live out our faith. Sometimes we get a little too far out on the ledge in life. We expose ourselves to spiritual and emotional harm by making poor choices. We remove our heart protection. We reject right relationships or righteousness and experiment dangerously.

There are a couple of things we need to do. We need to be around some people with whom we can be vulnerable. We need to let a few people protect our heart for us. We can tell them what is going on in our lives, share what is really happening with us.

As I discussed at length in an earlier chapter, I am not advocating putting on external behaviors. Our faith should lead to change taking place from the inside out in such a way that we develop "integrity of character." Integrity is defined in many ways—in terms of our sexual identity, our addictions, our affections, and so on. We are protected, we don't have a vulnerable spot. The breastplate is heart protection.

"Shoes for Good News" is the next piece of armor. One of the things Ephesians 6 says is that our feet should be "fitted with the readiness that comes from the gospel of peace." Ready for a long march? The shoes worn by the Roman army had nails coming out the bottoms for sound footing. They had a spike in the front for kicking in combat. A couple of major Roman victories took place because the Roman army had good shoes, which gave them good footing to move swiftly over mountain passes against their enemies.

We have to understand as Christians that the Good News of Jesus Christ becomes our foundation. In Christ we have solid footing. We can be ready to go anywhere. That means go to work, go home, go to church, and go out into the community. I know that my shoes are more comfortable going some places than others. I think all of us need to be challenged to be able to take the gospel of peace everywhere.

The shield of faith. It covers all the rest. After the soldiers were completely decked out in their armor, they were told, "You're covered, and here's the shield to double-cover you. It covers all the rest." Faith is wonderful that way. It's the thing that performs for us when we don't have other resources.

Too many of us face the battle somewhat naked. We wind up wounded. We are ill prepared to defend ourselves against "flaming arrows." The flaming arrows of which Paul speaks were arrows dipped in pine tar and ignited. They were on fire as they zoomed in at the enemy. It was a horrifying experience to be hit by one. Shields that were made of plain wood caught fire. Roman shields were covered with wet leather before battle so that when they were hit by fiery arrows the flames were extinguished. One of the things I see here is the need to carry our faith in front of us and believe God will give us resources to withstand challenges.

Another question. What if God packed up and left the church? Would we still be able to keep on doing what we have been doing? The answer, in most cases, is yes. We practice sound fiscal management and budgeting. We do everything in an organized way, according to the book. We always make sure the resources are there. God could get up and leave the church and we would just keep zipping along.

Actually, we should be positioned in such a way that if God deserted us we would be without hope. If our shield were removed, we would be right in the line of fire. We would be without resources and we would sink. Having the shield of faith in front of us—the belief that God will take care of "all the rest"—provides the crucial extra protection that we need.

The helmet of salvation. This is an interesting piece of armor. It was the only piece that wasn't self-installed. The soldier, by the time the helmet came along, had too much on. So the soldier's armor bearer would install the helmet. What a picture! Our salvation is something that we can't earn no matter how we do battle, no matter how we live our lives.

Our salvation is something that is handed to us to cover our head by our faith in Jesus Christ. It is a gift. God installs it. Many of us, including myself, live much of our lives coming up with schemes to cover our rear, rather than living the hope of salvation that covers our head. This is something that we need to focus on constantly—the hope of eternal life, and the fact that God has called each of us to be his beloved child.

The last part of the armor is the "sword of the Spirit, which is the word of God." Some people would argue that "the word of God" is a reference to Scripture. I don't think that is what it means in this context. I think it means that as we live in Christ, as we engage in our personal battles and external battles with the forces of evil in this world, God is prepared to give us a "word" for the situation.

For example, at a recent leadership meeting I attended, the unlikely subject of going to topless bars came up. We were talking about how things that seem somewhat innocuous can really pack a tremendous amount of evil in them. Now, none of us thought it was a good idea to go to such a bar. We all came to realize that there is a lot at stake here. You have to see it for what it really is.

If you see it as a little bit of sexual titillation and not very dangerous, just entertainment, that's one thing. But here is another way to look at it. Consider the person who dances at such a bar. Here is a child of God who for some reason has come across tough things in her life and found herself in a desperate situation. Now she disrobes on a stage and dances. But it is not just a dance. What you are watching is someone dying. She has been stripped of some of the comforts in life, taken advantage of, had her sense of dignity ripped from her. Many of the people who work at bars like this wind up on the streets, discarded. As a patron of this bar you are in the process of watching her die. I think God gives us clear vision for these types of situations to allow us to see things as they really are.

A final question. How do we fight? I think there are several ways. So please allow a consummate child of the sixties to impart some classic warfare strategies to you.

Infiltration. Infiltration is one of the greatest strategies of spiritual warfare that we have. Christians, rather than huddling together as Christians, find their source of strength in small groups. Then they infiltrate places like the media and the public schools. We begin to teach and to do our thing as God's people in the marketplace, in those parts of society that are hurting for a "word from God."

Subversion. Subversion brought about the end of slavery in America. Some people who had money and power began to subvert the system that bought and sold slaves. They undermined it by buying slaves and freeing them. Another example: A group of middle-aged women in the church where I serve are committed to visiting women who dance in topless clubs. They subversively begin to develop relationships with the dancers by offering unconditional love and acceptance. They give them back their dignity and help them get off the streets.

Guerrilla warfare. I love guerrilla warfare. It has a romantic and noble sound to it—for warfare. I see the ministry of Young Life as guerrilla warfare, as are outreach ministries to runaway kids in our inner-city areas. Guerrilla Christians dash into a situation, grab people where they are, and love them. They give them a chance to hear the Good News of Jesus Christ.

Flanking maneuvers. These are simply creative solutions to problems. In our society a lot of people are inclined to say, "Oh, there is no food or clothing for people who need it." Then there are others, like some people in my home church, who create food banks and clothing banks, and begin to feed the hungry and clothe the naked. This represents a sort of flanking maneuver—going around slow government systems. These folks are doing warfare, not just complaining about situations. They are finding new and creative solution to problems.

Frontal attack. Sometimes we need a direct offense. That means just lining up in a big row and charging. Sometimes we need to fight frontal-type wars in which we use the legal and social systems to overcome evil in our world. We see that happening right now in our society with issues like pornography, drugs, and homelessness.

If we have followed this pattern of Ephesians as depicted throughout the book, then we are learning to be strong in the Lord. We are growing and being changed from the inside. Further, the New Life in Christ is moving to the outside of us. It is inevitable that by such growth we will be led to outward encounters—encounters with our world's philosophies, systems, values, and institutions. There will be encounters with the world as a result of situations that we just can't stomach in the name of the gospel.

Let me encourage you to keep fighting when you fail. Not "if" you fail, but "when" you fail. The Roman poet Ovid said, "I see the better way and I approve it. But the worse one is the one I follow." All of us take that course at certain times. The apostle Paul said, "For what I want to do I do not do. . ." (Rom. 7:15b). We can all relate to the struggle with failure, but in spite of failure we need to keep on trying.

As we try and try again to live as God's people, we need to continue to ask God to give us eyes to see where the battles are, and courage and strength to pitch in. We must integrate our faith in Christ with our personal, social, and political beliefs. I'm not advocating any particular social or political position here. When someone comes up to me and argues against something, I am willing to accept that argument, even though I don't agree with it, if it is erected on a biblical foundation and on the person's faith in Christ. We need to base our view of the world on a biblical view, and we need to take up spiritual arms.

In Ephesians 6:13, Paul talks about the "day of evil." That phrase stands for the times when things are at their very worst. We have all faced days, weeks, and even months like that. Expect struggles. Expect to wrestle. Expect to get dirty in this world if you are going to live out your Christian faith. It cannot be avoided.

Finally, I want to encourage us all, in the midst of this, to remain in Christ. Jesus Christ is the focal point of the universe. We have to hang onto Christ and remember the words of G. Campbell Morgan, a great preacher of this century who said, "What we do in crisis always depends on whether we see difficulties in the light of God or in the shadow of the difficulties."

Afterword:
Undying Love

Peace to the brothers and sisters, and love with
faith from God the Father and the Lord Jesus
Christ. Grace to all who love our Lord Jesus
Christ with an undying love.

EPHESIANS 6:23-24

There is only one way before us that represents life—all other
options are just for killing time as life passes by. This way
to life is not easy. There will be pain. There will be fear and
disappointment. There will be failure. There will be joy.

The balance we need in order to live is incredible. We exist,
physically, on a very fine and uncertain edge. So it is with the
Christian life. Out of balance, we fling ourselves to one side, which
is the deadly fall to staid, legalistic religion—the lifeless, frozen religion that Jesus Christ came to abolish. In avoiding the fall to legalism, we encounter the danger of falling to the other side. That
side is the rubbish fire of cheap grace. Cheap grace applauds spiri-
tual-sounding phrases but takes all the bite—all the obligation, all
the discipleship—out of Christianity. It is useless. Jesus came to
abolish cheap grace, making it clear that when we reject God's will

and plans for our thoughts, words, and actions we are rejecting, not a system, but Jesus himself.

The only option that breeds life is the fine line of intimate and constant relationship with God the Father, the Lord Jesus Christ, and the Holy Spirit. This relationship permeates both our private lives and our lives in community with fellow believers and with the world at large. This is the place of grace and peace. This is the only place where true life happens.

A state of grace—the state of being gifted with all of God's resources—awaits those who will love the Lord Jesus Christ with an undying love. We are invited to a meaningful adventure.